SPORTS FUNDRAISING

Sports Fundraising is a complete introduction to fundamental principles and best practice in sports fundraising. Focusing on the particular challenges of fundraising in intercollegiate and interscholastic sport, and for youth sport organizations, the book is designed to help students develop the professional skills that they will need for a successful career in sports or education administration.

Packed with real-life case studies and scenarios, the book offers a step-by-step guide to the effective planning, communication, implementation and management of sports fundraising projects, and introduces the most important issues in contemporary sports fundraising. Each chapter contains a range of useful features, from definitions of key terms to skill building exercises, exploring both quantitative and qualitative methods for understanding the fundraising process and designing more effective fundraising projects. This is an essential text for any athletic or sport fundraising course, and an invaluable reference for all professional fundraisers working in sport or education.

David J. Kelley is an adjunct Assistant Professor in the newly created Sport Administration program at the University of Cincinnati, USA. Throughout his career, Dr Kelley successfully raised funds and secured grants to improve the sport programs under his supervision. He has published articles on sports fundraising, sponsorships, and curriculum development.

Sports Fundraising

Dynamic Methods for Schools, Universities and Youth Sport Organizations

David Kelley

LONDON AND NEW YORK

First published 2012
by Routledge
711 Third Avenue, New York, NY 10017

Simultaneously published in the USA and Canada
by Routledge
2 Park Square, Milton Park, Abingdon, Oxon OX14 4RN

Routledge is an imprint of the Taylor & Francis Group, an informa business

British Library Cataloguing in Publication Data
A catalogue record for this book is available from the British Library

Library of Congress Cataloging in Publication Data
Kelley, David J.
Sports fundraising : dynamic methods for schools, universities and youth sport organizations / edited by David Kelley. -- 1st ed.
p. cm.
1. Sports--Public relations. 2. Fund raising. 3. School sports--Finance. 4. College sports--Finance. I. Title.
GV714.K45 2012 659.2'9796--dc23
2011048985

ISBN: 978-0-415-50718-9 (hbk)
ISBN: 978-0-415-50719-6 (pbk)
ISBN: 978-0-203-12647-9 (ebk)

Typeset in Melior and Univers
by Bookcraft Limited, Stroud, Gloucestershire

CONTENTS

6 YOUTH AND INTERSCHOLASTIC RELATIONSHIP CULTIVATION AND STEWARDSHIP 83

7 LEVERAGING POINTS OF SALE AND PROFIT-MAKING FOR FUNDRAISING SUCCESS 109

8 WORKING WITH DIVERSE CONSTITUENCIES: CULTIVATION STRATEGIES AND ESSENTIAL RESOURCES 135

9 YOUTH/INTERSCHOLASTIC GRANTSMANSHIP: OPPORTUNITIES AND APPROACHES FOR SUCCESS **155**

10 THE FUTURE OF SPORTS FUNDRAISING: DATA-DRIVEN METHODOLOGIES AND CURRICULUM DEVELOPMENT IN HIGHER EDUCATION **172**

LIST OF FIGURES

PREFACE: THE PRIMARY PURPOSE OF THIS BOOK

This book was written primarily for students who are taking undergraduate and/or graduate coursework in Sport Management/Sport Administration programs or for those individuals who have been recently employed in interscholastic or intercollegiate athletic programs as practitioners. While it is nearly impossible to completely depict the body of knowledge that encompasses fundraising among all sports organizations in one book, *Sports Fundraising* is a collaborative and contemporary resource that addresses the need to provide creative, straightforward fundraising skills and guidelines coupled with ethical, intelligent application. Overall, those who read this book will be immersed into the exciting and challenging world of sports fundraising.

The primary purpose of this book is threefold. First is to provide both the student and practitioner the ability to identify and explain important principles, techniques, models, guidelines and specific challenges to effectively plan, communicate, implement and manage sports fundraising projects. Second is to develop the skills necessary to be a successful sports fundraiser through comprehending the various fundraising methods, models and principles by practicing the various application/skill building exercises throughout the book. The third purpose is to develop the ability to apply all of the practical knowledge in an ethical and professional manner.

Overall, merely reading this book will not make you a great sports fundraiser. As with learning any new skill, it takes practice. Finally, if the concepts and exercises in this book are taken in earnest, those individuals will be better equipped to create and manage significant revenue streams into their youth sport, interscholastic or intercollegiate athletic departments.

ACKNOWLEDGEMENTS

This book is dedicated to my wife, Tami, and our children Miranda and Sean, who have been supportive, open-minded and encouraging throughout the extensive hours of research and preparation for this book.

A very special acknowledgement goes to my parents Francis and Margaret Kelley. I cherish the eternal love and support you have provided me and want you both to know how much I appreciate it. For their unending love and support of my passion, I dedicate this book.

I would also like to acknowledge Bob Arkeilpane and Greg Stanley, both of whom were very generous with sharing their time, experience, ideas and insights on fundraising. I respect their perspectives and without them, this book would not have been possible to complete. I also want to thank M.B. Reilly, who was very accommodating and helped facilitate moving forward with this project, thank you. To Eric Horstman for his assistance with this project, Dr Joe Young for his professionalism and efforts as a reviewer and Dr Curt Laird for his personal and professional friendship in addition to his contributions as a reviewer, a special thank-you as well.

Finally, to my mentors, Dr Andrew Kreutzer and Professor Bob Brinkmeyer, your continued guidance, support and assistance in my career are greatly appreciated. Both of you exemplify and model the kind of professionalism I desire and as such, I value our relationship.

CHAPTER 1

SPORTS FUNDRAISING: CHALLENGES AND PREREQUISITES

The purpose of this chapter is to focus attention to the youth sport, interscholastic and intercollegiate athletic domains. Additionally, an overview of the various challenges and contemporary dynamics faced by these organizations, relative to an ever-changing economic climate, will be examined.

INTRODUCTION

Youth, interscholastic and intercollegiate sports are extremely popular in the United States. Commonly referred to as *Little League* and/or *Pee Wee Sports*, *High School Sports* or *Athletics*, and *College Sports* or *Athletics*, the popularity of this significant phenomenon is evidenced primarily in the participation rates as well as the increased televising of events. For example, The Walt Disney Company's ESPN Inc. created a channel devoted entirely to college sports. According to the ESPN website (n.d.) ESPNU came on the scene on 4 March 2005, and has grown to cover not only a multitude of college sports, but also youth and high school sports programming. In 2006, ESPN contracted with Little League Baseball to provide live televised coverage of the entire 32-game tournament for an eight-year period. Moreover, ESPN Inc. launched *ESPN RISE Magazine*, which has evolved into a multimedia phenomenon for the promotion of high school sports content across a wide variety of mediums and events. In August 2011, ESPN Inc. introduced *ESPN High School*, which made its television debut on the ESPN High School Football Kickoff, 26–28 August 2011. Simultaneous to this multimedia boom, interest and participation rates have continued to escalate among youth, high school and college athletic programs across the United States as well. Consequently, Kelley asserts, "It would appear that the monies needed to administer these programs has not kept up with the growth of popularity in such programs and their participation rates" (2002, p.1).

Whether it is due to the inadequate budget allocations for athletics or the pressure to do more with less, fundraising has and will continue to be a challenge at all levels of competition. Therefore, program offerings and expansion is a reality and as such, seeking new revenue streams to aid in funding them is no longer just recommended, it is a required skill set that sport administrators must possess in today's society. This book will aid in facilitating the appreciation and comprehension of fundraising at the youth, interscholastic and intercollegiate levels.

Unlike any other textbook on fundraising, the objective is not just to be read, understood and then filed away on a bookshelf. Rather, this textbook is a hands-on and skill acquisition resource that is intended to facilitate ongoing examination from both a practical and experimental perspective.

CHALLENGES AT THE YOUTH SPORT LEVEL

Youth sport programs are very popular activities in the United States, as has been previously illustrated. Youth sport programs across the United States are usually organized by, for example:

- local community centers and recreation departments
- YMCAs and YWCAs
- private youth sports clubs
- nationally sponsored non-profit youth sport organizations
- Boys and Girls Clubs of America.

Significant amounts of research and empirical analysis into the problematic features of youth sport in terms of participation and dropout rates, commercialization issues, supervision and competency issues among volunteer coaches, and an over-emphasis on competition and winning over fundamental instruction and development are just a few examples of these areas of inquiry. Consequently, research has been lacking in the area of *youth sports fundraising* in comparison to the other areas. The contemporary dynamics and challenges of youth sport administration have heightened the need for fundraising. These dynamics include, but are not limited to, the following components:

- a lack of trained athletic administrators in the youth sport environment
- an over-reliance on school- and community-owned athletic facilities
- limited financial assistance from communities to support youth sport programs
- parental involvement as youth sport administrators and booster club representatives
- competition from other non-profit youth sport organizations and faith-based organizations
- competition from for-profit youth sport organizations.

In many instances, youth sport programs have a significant reliance, and in some cases a dependency, on city and/or community recreational facilities as well as city and/or community school district athletic facilities. The financial sources of paying for the use of these athletic facilities are largely from state government parks and recreation budget allocations, school district budget allocations, parents paying program fees, private donations and fundraising activities. The costs associated with operating athletic facilities in terms of maintenance, operational costs, custodial care of outdoor playing surfaces and gymnasiums are a significant reason why fundraising is necessary. There is a very alarming trend in youth sport administration, according to the National Alliance for Youth Sports, hereafter known as NAYS. They report "an estimated 70 percent of all youth sport programs are operated by parent-interest groups, which use public facilities that are provided through community tax dollars" (2011, p.7).

Youth sports provide many great opportunities for children to develop their sport skills as well as their socialization skills, among the myriad of other benefits of participation. However, because many youth sports programs are organized and financed by parent-interest groups, an unfortunate part of this arrangement has led to the physical and emotional turmoil of children. For example, NAYS (2011, p.7) explains that these youth sport leagues "are administered by adults, whose own motives, morals, and beliefs influence, to varying degrees, how the program is conducted." For the most part, these are the same parents who are dissatisfied with community-based sport organizations such as YMCAs/YWCAs or Boys and Girls Clubs who have rules and policies in place that ensure equal playing time in addition to positively enhancing children's physical, mental and social development. As a result, these parent-interest groups create their own leagues that have their own rules and regulations where the *best players* play, and the concept of equal playing time for every child is snubbed.

There is an ever-increasing *culture* of parents who, as spectators, ridicule game officials as well as take on the role of youth coaches. For the most part, they are untrained and/ or incompetent coaches. Consequently, they are competing for space in many community recreation centers and school district sport facilities across the United States. To make matters worse, budgets that previously allocated monies to parks and recreation have been cut drastically over the years as well as budget cuts to school district athletic programs. Therefore, as NAYS explains, "the perception that parents using public facilities are in some way an extension of the local program is often incorrect" (2011, p.7). On top of those issues, as time progresses, the cost of sports equipment, facility rental, uniforms are among a variety of programmatic costs that continue to escalate due to economic inflation.

The good news is that most of the millions of volunteers across the United States, who administer, coach and perhaps referee or umpire youth sports, do indeed have the best of intentions and are involved for the right reasons. However, first and foremost, the *lack of training* appears to be the common denominator that is afflicting youth sports. Much of the professional literature on youth sport focuses on the parent-interest groups that expose children to the physical and emotional risks and rightfully so. Moreover, when it comes to fundraising, the approaches implemented by these parent-interest groups are frequently unplanned, disorganized, and unoriginal.

Philosophically, the youth sport organizational structure is distorted and as such, needs professionally trained individuals to assume the roles that have been fulfilled by the parent-interest groups. NAYS is a non-profit organization that promotes the values and importance of sports and attempts to provide positive opportunities and experiences for children. They also provide training for volunteers and organizational administrators concerning the impact that sport has on the emotional, physical and social development of youth. In a document that they developed to help raise the standards of community youth sport programs and the detrimental behaviors plaguing youth sports, they provide *education and accountability* standards for youth sport administrators. Educational topics that NAYS recommends include: "Philosophy of children's sports, managing parents, managing volunteers, managing conflict, risk management and fund raising" (2011, p.26). As such, there is adequate evidence to suggest that the lack of financial resources combined with the lack of formalized training is tainting youth sports at all levels.

The current methods of fundraising in youth sport lack a proactive, organized, imaginative and mission-driven orientation. For the most part, youth sports fundraising has been characterized by parents and children pushing products such as merchant-discount coupon cards, pre-paid debit cards or some type of candy onto the community in an unorganized and in some cases, relentless manner. Typically, this creates aggravation for both the youth sport organization and community as a whole. Therefore, these types of fundraisers usually fall short of their intended goals and as a result, fundraising frustration develops.

In sum, those who read this book need to be open-minded to the possibilities and methodologies this book has to offer. Ultimately, this will aid in identifying and addressing significant fundraising obstacles by helping those who care about and are involved in youth sport.

CHALLENGES AT THE INTERSCHOLASTIC LEVEL

In order to operate an efficient and effective athletic program at the interscholastic level, there are numerous reasons why fundraising is necessary. The four principal reasons are as follows:

- school district budgetary allocations for athletics are inadequate
- new technology within the sports equipment, facilities and sport surface industry that the school wants or needs to purchase
- the pressure to do more with less
- managing public perception of the athletic program.

First, school district budgetary allocations for athletics are inadequate. In many schools across the country, most budgetary allocations can range from two percent or less of the school district's overall budget. In most instances, that two percent or less must be stretched to cover the costs of the entire athletic program's expenses. The rising costs of various components ranging from purchasing sports equipment, contracting game officials, individual sport expenses to transportation costs and instructional/coaching salaries are just a few of the areas which that budget allocation covers.

Second, the contemporary dynamic of technological advances within the sports equipment, facilities and sport surface industries. For example, there are new artificial sports surfaces that are multipurpose, versatile, and can withstand the wear and tear of numerous sporting activities compared to natural surfaces. While these new surfaces can prove to be cost-effective in the long-term, they are for the most part, very expensive. Additionally, even though the longevity of the surfaces is relatively unknown, most companies that install the product generally have an eight- to ten-year warranty and simultaneously promote the savings compared to natural grass surfaces. As a result, fundraising becomes an essential undertaking to cover the costs associated with any kind of technological innovation that an interscholastic athletic department considers significant.

The third challenge is the pressure to do more with less. For example, in many instances around the United States, the athletic facilities are outdated, old and/or too small. What was once appropriate in the 1970s or 1980s is now insufficient to accommodate the needs of the athletic program because of the changes in the number of athletic activities offered on account of enrollment patterns and participation rates based on student interest. As a result, athletic directors are forced to *do more with less* in terms of scheduling and managing athletic facilities that were constructed to reflect the enrollment patterns of the past twenty or thirty years.

According to the National Federation of State High School Athletic Associations, otherwise known as the NFHS, the data from their website is based on figures from the fifty state high school athletic/activity associations, plus those in the District of Columbia, that are members of the NFHS. Participation for the 2010–11 school year rose by 39,578 students to 7,667,955, compared to the 2009–10 High School Athletics Participation Survey conducted by the NFHS. An NFHS press release explains, "'While the overall increase was not as much as we've seen in the past few years, we are definitely encouraged with these totals given the financial challenges facing our nation's high schools,' said Bob Gardner, NFHS Executive Director". Moreover, Gardner suggested in the press release that, "The benefits of education-based athletics at the high school level are well-documented, and we encourage communities throughout the nation to keep these doors of opportunity open" (2011, p.1). Based on these statistics, if the number of students participating in high school athletics in the United States continues at the rate displayed above, by 2015 the overall participation rate should be reasonably close to eight million student athletes. Consequently, it is anticipated that program offerings and expansion are a reality and this will ultimately lead to seeking new revenue streams to aid in funding them.

Finally, another challenging component to fundraising at the interscholastic level is the management of public perception. There are many supporters of athletic programs and there are also critics. In general, the critics can come from many disciplines, but when it comes to raising funds, conversations ultimately will gravitate toward whether or not *taxes* will come into play. In this instance, even the most highly organized and efficient fundraising campaign, which is only soliciting private donations for an interscholastic athletic department for a public school system, can potentially be weakened by unsubstantiated communication. Therefore, the prudent athletic administrator takes this into consideration as an anticipated challenge, if the fundraising initiative is to be carried out in an effective and efficient manner.

Overall, there are many other challenges facing interscholastic athletic programs across the United States relative to the costs associated with managing a program, such as pay-to-play initiatives, booster organizations, corporate sponsorships as well as a multitude of other fundraising techniques that will be covered throughout the book.

CHALLENGES AT THE INTERCOLLEGIATE LEVEL

Intercollegiate and interscholastic athletic programs both share similar pressures outlined above, however, intercollegiate athletic programs and the fundraising activities they utilize are associated more as having dual elements of *return on investment strategies* such as contracted business arrangements with specific marketing and profit-making objectives as well as *philanthropy*, compared to interscholastic programs. Some of the more specific contemporary dynamics faced by intercollegiate athletic programs can include, but are not limited to:

- the economy
- the emergence of various public relations/press mediums
- tax laws – IRS restrictions
- corporate matching gift programs
- an over-saturation of charitable organizations/worthy causes in the marketplace.

Additionally, when the economy is in turmoil, people look at areas to cut back their disposable income. In general, charitable gifts often get reduced or cut altogether and that has a direct impact on sports fundraising efforts. Mediums such as talk radio, Internet sites, message boards, chat rooms and blogs can produce an accumulation of negativity. For example, there are many outstanding athletic programs in the United States at the intercollegiate level. Yet, anyone who is dissatisfied with a specific athletic program or even a particular coach can create a website on the Internet so they can vent their frustrations and allow others to participate in the form of a blog, chat room or e-mail blast. Furthermore, the aforementioned blogs, chat rooms and Internet sites are an information type of medium that is part of the athletic landscape. These mediums can negatively impact sports fundraising efforts as well. As a result, these forums have the power to not only affect people's perceptions of your athletic program, but also impact how money is raised. Athletics is an area in which the entirety of a gift is not 100 percent tax-deductible as it is with other non-profit organizations. If a donor is receiving a benefit in return (i.e. premium tickets, preferred parking space) for their donation and there is a *quid pro quo*, then there are rules established by the United States IRS (Internal Revenue Service) that restrict the donation from being 100 percent tax-deductible. Based on IRS rules, if the donor receives the right to purchase a seat or preferred seating in return for their gift, then only eighty percent of their contribution is tax-deductible. Furthermore, donors should be made aware of this tax rule *prior* to making their donation. Consequently, donors can elect to decline priority seating and other benefits and as a result, deduct 100 percent of their contribution if they so choose.

Among the various companies/corporations in which people work, often the company will match a gift to the charitable organization to which the employee chooses to contribute. Often, athletics is restricted and companies will not match those types of gifts, which can be a challenge at the intercollegiate level. Most companies require that the donor not receive any goods or services in relation to a gift. Otherwise, upon proper verification and human resource guidelines, most companies will match a gift at a 1:1 ratio.

In general, most Americans have only a certain portion of their disposable income to gift. Furthermore, there are a plethora of good and worthy causes and everyone who works for those charitable organizations is out there soliciting for those disposable monies. For example, the non-profit sector has a significant number of charitable organizations whose mission and purpose are to improve the lives of the people they serve and as such, they provide compelling cases for support. As a result, in a personal conversation with University of Cincinnati Deputy Director of Athletics, Bob Arkeilpane, he indicated that "there is an *over-saturation* of charitable organizations and worthy causes in the marketplace" (2009) which makes fundraising at the intercollegiate athletic level even more challenging. As stated earlier, one of the primary differences between fundraising at the intercollegiate level in comparison to youth and interscholastic athletic programs is that they are more ROI (*return on investment*) as well as philanthropic in their orientation. Furthermore, the size and scope of the organizations themselves relative to their resources, both human and financial, are other facets that differentiate college programs from youth and interscholastic athletic programs. In general, interscholastic athletic programs have the administrative oversight of a Director of Athletics and support staff. Respectively, the size and scope of even the smallest of intercollegiate athletic programs are, for the most part, larger than an interscholastic athletic program with a significantly large enrollment.

Certainly, there are exceptions to the rule; however, even the largest of interscholastic athletic programs generally do not have full-time staff members with the title of Assistant Athletic Director for Marketing/ Promotions, Sports Information Director, Assistant Athletic Director of Development/Fundraising, Assistant Athletic Director of Facilities/ Operations, or even the Assistant Athletic Director for Compliance and Student Services. Nevertheless, despite these differences in terms of size and philosophic orientation, when it comes to raising funds, there are fundamental principles, techniques, models, guidelines and challenges to effectively plan, communicate, implement and manage that are applicable at all three levels and that are the rationale behind this book.

Furthermore, there are strategies and techniques from the intercollegiate athletic domain which the youth and interscholastic athletic programs in the United States could adopt in order to anticipate and manage the previously mentioned contemporary financial challenges they face.

FUNDRAISING PREREQUISITES

First, a *mission statement*, a brief statement that identifies and describes the ideals, beliefs and overall philosophy that guide the entire athletic organization. In general, there are a variety of mission statements throughout interscholastic and intercollegiate athletic programs, some good and others not so good. For example, there are mission statements that state: *XYZ University's intercollegiate athletic program is a genuine extension of secondary school programs, offering competent student athletes the opportunity to advance their development beyond high school.* This is not a mission statement; it is a goal or purpose statement. All too often, there are numerous mission statements crafted in this fashion. Seiler affirms, "Any statement containing an infinitive phrase – *to deliver, to serve, to provide* – is a goal or purpose statement, telling what the organization does" (2003, p.53). A mission statement is supposed to provide an explanation as to *why* the organization does what it does. Words and phrases that emphasize "We value" or begin with "It is our belief that" more appropriately explain why the athletic program exists. For instance: *At XYZ University, we believe in developing the full potential of our student athletes. The entire athletic program values unity, academic achievement, ethical conduct, sportsmanship and the judicious management of resources. Because we care about student athletes, the athletic department provides for the physical, mental and social needs of our student athletes so that they can compete and succeed academically and athletically ...* This brief example more appropriately explains *why* XYZ University does what it claims to do. Ideally, in developing a mission statement, acquiring input from employees, volunteers/boosters and other stakeholders is vitally important to help focus and clearly define exactly what the athletic program believes in accomplishing.

In sum, when the mission statement is created and articulated in this fashion, it will aid in providing the fundamental rationale for supporting the athletic program, especially when it comes to fund-raising initiatives. Consequently, goals and/or purpose statements are generalized intentions and as such, are not easy to measure. Instead, goals/purpose statements serve to guide the organization to carry out the beliefs and/or values verbalized in the mission statement. Objectives are the specific steps or the more precise *road map* that explains how the organization anticipates attaining its shared goals. Moreover, in crafting objectives, the SMART acronym is a key procedure. Seiler explains SMART stands for "*specific, measurable, achievable, results-oriented, and time-determined*" (2003, p.53). In this instance, the *goal* may be to increase the size of the athletic booster club and as such, the *objectives* illustrate how that will be achieved. A statement such as *we will increase athletic booster club membership by ten percent during the next calendar year* incorporates the SMART procedure. As with any other initiative, proper organization is a key element in fundraising, yet having an understanding and appreciation of the factors that can impact fundraising prior to organizing/rallying support is just as important. Clearly, articulating an appropriately crafted mission statement which is accompanied by well-thought-out goals and SMART objectives is one prerequisite for successful fundraising at all three levels.

Another prerequisite or key concept to be understood and appreciated involves identifying and developing a *constituency*. A constituency, by definition, is any united group of people who share similar goals and have a common sense of destiny. The term is used frequently in the political arena.

In other instances these are referred to as *stakeholders* or *centers of influence*. Timothy Seiler (2003) developed a model to represent this phenomenon (see Figure 1.1). Additionally, while this model was developed for the institutional fundraising domain, and is primarily used by those in university advancement and development, the implications of utilizing and effectively integrating this model into the athletics fundraising field are quite evident and highly

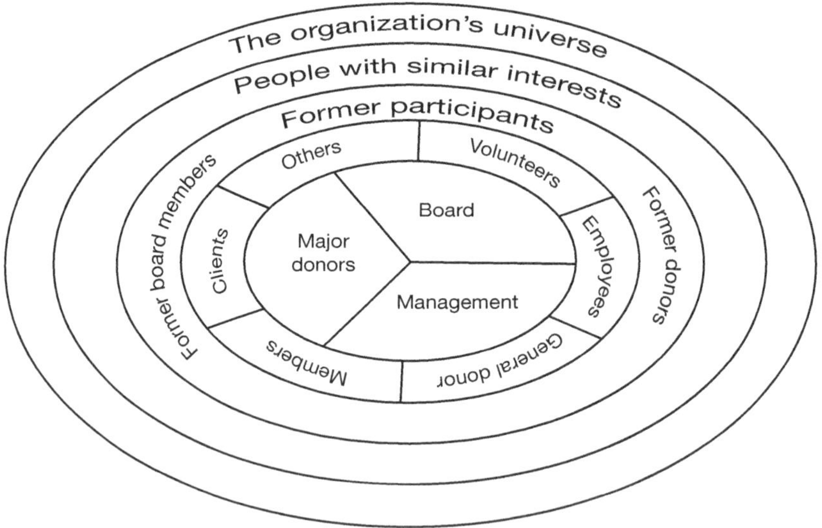

Figure 1.1 The Constituency Model

Source: Rosso, H. A. (2003) *Achieving Excellence in Fundraising* (2nd edn), San Francisco, CA: Jossey-Bass, p. 42

recommended. Seiler states "Schools, colleges and universities, for example, have students and alumni. Many educational institutions expand their constituencies to include parents and grandparents of current students. Hospitals have patients, often referred to in fundraising circles as grateful patients. Arts organizations have patrons, members, and audiences" (2003, p.41). In fundraising for youth, interscholastic and/or intercollegiate athletic programs, there are some *natural constituencies* to consider as well as other constituencies that are not as natural or easy to identify as described above. These are people who perhaps are former athletes, school district personnel or even school district administrators who support athletics. In addition, it could be a member of the community who has an innate interest in the athletic program and attends games/contests on a regular basis.

Overall, identifying and developing the people who currently are, who were, or who will potentially be, involved with the athletic program need to be carefully considered as part of the constituency because they are the prospects that are most likely to donate money to the athletic program. It is very important to take the time and effort to identify and create a positive alliance between the constituency and the athletic program. To better understand the overall *gist* of the constituency model, a visual representation of the way in which the *energy* of an organization is distributed needs to be explained.

The very core of the model represents *the highest level of energy*. The higher the energy, the stronger the bond is to the organization. As it travels outward, the successive circles become larger yet weaker in their energy and bond to the organization. A key principle of the model to understand is that the highest level of energy is at the core and subsequently flows outward. Effective fundraising must commence with the people in the core circle and be taken to the outer circles by those people. Another key principle of this model to understand and appreciate is "fluidity in the circles" (Seiler 2003, p.44). For example, maybe there is a change in the management and a new Athletic Director needs to be hired. Perhaps a *platinum level* donor to your athletic program one year may, for whatever reason, decide to only be a *bronze level* donor the next year. The disposable income of people may change due to the economy or a donor may change their career path. Seiler suggests that "Patterns in constituency development show that a 20 to 25 percent change annually is to be expected" (2003, p.44).

Consequently, the prudent sports administrator needs to be cognizant and responsive to the fact that not only is there *fluidity* of change among the elements that make up each circle, but that there is also constant interaction within and between the constituency circles. How effective a sport organization is at identifying, cultivating and ultimately attracting people closer and closer to the center will largely depend upon how well they *connect* and pay attention to the needs and values of the constituents, which will help draw them into the mission of the organization. Certainly a *winning program* will have a significant influence on fundraising. However, despite factors like winning and losing, the essential concept to keep in mind here is the issues and/or circumstances related to the money that is needed to sustain a quality athletic program, regardless of the win–loss record. For instance, previous empirical research published in 2008 by Shapiro indicated that while donations and gifts to college athletic departments were primarily motivated by benefits such as priority seating at football and basketball games, it will only yield short-term benefits if priority ticket allocations are tied too closely to team success. Shapiro explains, "If athletic departments rely too much on this approach, and the football and men's basketball teams are not successful, then the value of tickets will decrease along with the motivation for charitable contributions" (2008, p.118).

Thus, a mission-based relationship-building strategy that provides more than ticket or parking benefits, as Shapiro points out, "will help maintain a consistent source of fundraising that is not directly influenced by the frequent changes in individual team success" (2008, p.118).

Furthermore, the reality has been well documented as Howard and Crompton explain: "College athletics is far from its popular perception as a 'cash cow' for higher education. Spiraling costs, increased competition, and flat or declining revenues have all combined to place intercollegiate sports programs under severe financial pressure" (2004, p.22). Whether these factors are based upon inadequate budget allocations, technological advances in the sport industry or even the concept of doing more with less from an athletic programming standpoint, the reality is that these financial obstacles will never go away.

Overall, there are a variety of challenges that will continue to test the athletic director's creativity, tenacity and entrepreneurial spirit. As such, creativity and the aggressive pursuit of alternative funding sources are not merely desirable, but imperative for the majority of youth, high school and college athletic organizations across the United States. Ultimately, these are requisite skill sets for the contemporary athletic administrator to not only comprehend, but to be proficient in.

FURTHER READING

Biddle, B. J. and Berliner, D. C. (2002) "What research says about unequal funding for schools in America", *Policy Perspectives*, available at www.eric.ed.gov/PDFS/ED473409.pdf (accessed 01/31/12).

Burch, P. (2009) *Hidden markets: The new education privatization*, New York: Routledge.

Culbertson, B. K. (2008) "Supplementing annual school district budgets: Partnerships, fundraisers, foundations, and local support venues", University of North Texas, available at http://search.proquest.com/docview/304537768?accountid=2909 (accessed 01/31/12).

Gladden, J. M., Mahoney, D. F. and Apostolopoulou, A. (2005) "Toward a better understanding of college athletic donors: What are the primary motives?" *Sport Marketing Quarterly* 14 (1) 18–30.

Hedstrom, R. and Gould, D. (2004) "Research in youth sports: Critical issues status: Institute for the study of youth sport", Michigan State University, available at http://www.educ.msu.edu/ysi/project/CriticalIssuesYouthSports.pdf (accessed 01/31/12).

Kanters, M. (2002) "Parents and youth sports", *Parks and Recreation*, 37 (12) 20–28.

Nicholson, B. L. (2010) "The commercialization of youth sport and its implications for privatization in education", University of California, Berkeley, available at http://search.proquest.com/docview/859003684?accountid=2909 (accessed 01/31/12).

Popke, M. (2010) "Booster Clubs are Saving High School Sports", *Athletic Business*, available at http://athleticbusiness.com/articles/article.aspx?articleid=3618&zoneid=35 (accessed 01/31/12).

Rosso, H. A. (2003) *Achieving Excellence in Fundraising* (2nd edn), San Francisco, CA: Jossey-Bass.

Schnoes, D. J. (2008) "The perceptions about youth sport programs in Nebraskan communities", University of Nebraska, available at http://search.proquest.com/docview/89267722?accountid=2909 (accessed 01/31/12).

Sharp, W., Malone, B. and Walter, J. (2003) "Superintendent Observations Regarding the Financial Condition of their School Districts: A Three-State Study", available at http://www.eric.ed.gov/PDFS/ED481620.pdf (accessed 01/31/12).

Tsiotsou, R. (2004) "The role of involvement and income in predicting small and large donations to college athletics", *International Journal of Sports Marketing & Sponsorship*, 6 (2) 117–123.

—— (2006) "Investigating differences between female and male athletic donors: A comparative study", *International Journal of Nonprofit and Voluntary Sector Marketing*, 11 (3) 209–223.

Warwick, M. (2000) *The five strategies for fundraising success: A mission-based guide to achieving your goals*, San Francisco, CA: Jossey-Bass.

Zimmer, R., Krop, C., Kaganoff, T., Ross, K. E. and Brewer, D. (2001) "Private Giving to Public Schools and Districts in Los Angeles County: A Pilot Study", Santa Monica, CA: Rand, available at http://www.rand.org/pubs/monograph_reports/MR1429.html (accessed 01/31/12).

APPLICATION/SKILL BUILDING EXERCISE

Exercise applicable for both students and practitioners

Select a youth sport organization, a high school and a college/university of your choice to examine/study. Get on the Internet and browse the school's website. Most public institutions post their mission statements. In some instances, the athletic department's website/web page is separate from that of the institution and as such, you may need to browse a separate link to view the athletic department's website/web page. Based on the chapter lesson on *fundraising prerequisites*, try and answer the following questions:

- Does the youth sport organization, the athletic departments of the high school or the college/university have their mission statement posted?
- If so, does the mission statement provide an appropriate explanation as to why the youth sport organization exists? Or why the high school and college athletic department exists? Or, does the posted mission statement provide an explanation of what the youth organization/athletic department does?

Based on the information you gathered (or if there was no mission statement posted):

1. Would you change/modify the mission statement?
2. If you would change/modify it, identify the areas you would change and rewrite it.
3. If you wouldn't change/modify it, explain why, and explain how you determined that the mission statement was well crafted.
4. If there wasn't one posted, create/write a mission statement based on what you learned in this chapter.

CHAPTER 2

FUNDRAISING ORGANIZATION

The purpose of this chapter is to focus attention to the reasons for booster clubs, and their organizational dynamics. Organizational hierarchy of booster clubs at the youth, high school and collegiate level will be addressed as well as contemporary issues related to the oversight of these support groups with specific examples. Finally, an analysis concerning booster club fundraising methodologies and the importance of gender equity toward advancing compliance will be reviewed.

As detailed in Chapter 1, sport programs at the youth, high school and collegiate levels are faced with the realities of popularity and increased participation rates which, in turn, creates the need for external financial support. There are a diverse number of reasons why there is a real need for booster clubs, and some of these reasons include, but are not limited to, the following components:

- deficient budget allocations from the educational institution
- the costs associated with new technology within the sports equipment, facilities and sport surface industry
- program expansion based on participation rates
- economic inflation
- the escalation of spending to hire, retain, and supervise high-caliber personnel
- the incremental escalation of insurance costs (liability and medical).

Therefore, booster clubs, also known as *external support groups*, are needed and will continue to be needed to raise the funds to not only supplement certain sports/activities, but in many cases, help ensure their survival.

WHY SCHOOLS NEED BOOSTER CLUBS

Across the United States, for a myriad of reasons, the financial allocation from many of the educational institutions to support interscholastic and intercollegiate athletic programs has significantly diminished. Those diminished dollars translate into cutbacks in operational supplies, equipment, and transportation, just to name a few. When the institution cuts the budget to the extent that it can cover only a portion of the coaching salaries, uniforms and supplies needed to operate, the following are examples of what may get sacrificed: appropriate medical supervision, up-to-date athletic equipment/protective gear, proper maintenance of athletic fields and facilities, the costs associated with transporting teams to the away contests, and liability insurance premiums. As a result of these budget shortfalls, the number of sports teams and/or specific activities within the sport are severely cut back or eliminated altogether. For example, there are many school districts in the United States that offer Track & Field. The pole vault, based on the inherent risk of the activity, can be too costly from an insurance standpoint for the schools' athletic departments to offer. Therefore, while various other events such as running and jumping are offered, the pole vault has been eliminated as an event from the athletic program in many instances. In other cases, the entire sport or team has been eliminated. Ice hockey is a sport that not only has inherent risks associated with the activity (including increasing insurance premiums), but also has the *cost of doing business*, such as paying for up-to-date protective gear and equipment, ice rink facility rental and the transportation costs, all of which make ice hockey a very expensive sport to administer.

As the United States entered into the new millennium, new technological developments emerged, and we quickly entered into the *age of technology* that saw an explosion of people using the Internet as a social networking medium, as well as other computer aided technologies. Concurrent to this technological phenomenon was the creative innovation of the sports equipment, facilities and sport surface industries. From the introduction of full body swimsuits made of polyurethane that simultaneously reduces hydrodynamic drag and increases buoyancy, to stadiums constructed with high-definition multimedia scoreboards, to the colossal interest in multi-purpose artificial grass with a ground-rubber compost, technological advancement in sport has incrementally redefined the arms race for the latest and greatest technology. Moreover, the price to acquire the latest swimsuits, golf clubs, football helmets, scoreboards or multi-purpose artificial sports surface is, in most cases, beyond the financial scope of the athletic budget, yet, is exactly within the domain of the booster club.

When analyzing the impact of the United States economy compared to the increased participation rates in both interscholastic and intercollegiate sports, we discern an intriguing dynamic that appears to have had an *inverse relationship* over the last three decades. This is another reason why there is a significant need for booster clubs. For example, interscholastic athletics has had participation rates increase over the last thirty years and continues to climb, as was detailed in Chapter 1. Simultaneously, the monies spent to support these programs during the same time period has been severely cut back. As a result, the astute sport administrator needs not only to be cognizant of this reality, but also be able to cultivate financial support for survival. There are numerous examples of high school athletic programs, coast-to-coast in the United States, that are fighting to stay alive because in times when the economy is stagnant, public support for school tax levies falls short or often fails. In reaction to this tough economic landscape, many schools initiated pay-to-play and/or user fees. In some areas of the country, transportation to athletic contests was limited to no more than a fifty-mile radius from the school district; otherwise, the contest was canceled.

While efforts by the cheerleaders, soccer team, football team or band members such as washing cars, or selling candy, pre-paid debit cards or gift-wrap are a *fact of life* in many athletic programs throughout the country, this should only be viewed as one small piece of the fundraising puzzle and should be used judiciously. This is where the support and dedication of the booster club comes into play as they solicit private donations and corporate support for the entire athletic program. Residents, merchants and other businesses in the community are constantly being asked for support/donations. If carried out in a well-planned/orchestrated fundraising drive at specific times during the year, this can lead to more success by *teaming up* the needs of the cheerleaders, soccer team, football team as well as other teams instead of having those groups/teams solicit funds in a fragmented fashion.

Another contemporary dynamic that has had a significant impact on the finances among both interscholastic and intercollegiate athletic programs is the escalation of spending to hire, retain and supervise high-caliber personnel. At the thirty-first National Conference of High School Athletic Directors in San Diego, California, that was presented by the National Federation of State High School Associations (NFHS), an empirical study was completed to analyze the administrative tasks/duties interscholastic athletic directors perform. Among the many results, the top ten most important tasks/duties interscholastic athletic directors perform was determined; the most important being identified as *recruiting and supervising coaches* (Kelley 2002). Additionally, the financial resources needed to carry out this vitally important obligation have significantly escalated, especially when athletic department budgets are already being stretched to meet the programmatic demands beyond salaries and benefits.

In general, the cost associated with hiring high-caliber personnel is an economic process that includes but is not limited to:

- Recruiting costs: these can include classified advertising costs, screening resumes, telephone and time costs to set appointments, interviewing costs, and mail correspondence costs for thank-you letters and rejection letters.
- Personnel costs: these can include the multiple hours of lost productivity due to the time required for hiring activities, the direct financial cost if a third party is used as the hiring authority, and the cost due to the amount of time away from focusing on the goals of the organization.
- Training costs: these can include the direct cost of the classes and/or certification(s) the new employee must have/take at the expense of the organization, the indirect costs to the organization associated with having an inexperienced person on the job versus an experienced person, and the indirect cost of lost productivity due to the orientation of the new hire.
- Turnover costs: this combines the personal costs and the training costs due to there being a thirty-five to fifty percent chance of having turnover when taking a candidate from the pool of unemployed. Added all together in terms of the direct recruiting costs, the total personnel costs and total training and turnover costs are

quite significant and can be very expensive, especially in times of economic instability.

Another area that has a significant impact on the finances of both interscholastic and intercollegiate athletic programs is the incremental escalation of insurance costs for both liability insurance and medical insurance coverage. This is an area that can literally eliminate participation opportunities because the expense of covering the risk is too great for the athletic program/school system to take on.

For a variety of reasons, some schools face the dilemma of encouraging participation, yet are unable to provide the opportunity due to the increasing insurance coverage costs. In many interscholastic athletic programs, specific activities within sports or even the sport itself have been eliminated from the program due to the high risk associated with the activity and/or the sport itself. As mentioned previously, the athletic event of pole vaulting in Track & Field has been eliminated as well as many ice hockey programs. Football is a sizable expense and as such, many schools/universities have eliminated football from their athletic programs.

The care and overall *wellness* of student athletes is a high priority, and rightfully so. Consequently, the cost of annual insurance coverage premiums for the care, treatment and rehabilitation of athletes has escalated. Among many youth, interscholastic and intercollegiate athletic programs over the last thirty years, athletes who desired to participate in sports had to provide their own individual insurance coverage because the school districts and/or universities were forced to eliminate athletic insurance coverage. Thus, depending on the liability associated with the sporting activities themselves, the prudent athletic administrator needs to be aware of the *costs* of medical and liability insurance. Furthermore, based on this knowledge, they must decide whether or not to transfer the risk to a third party or if they need to eliminate the sport/activity altogether.

Booster clubs are needed and will continue to be needed to raise the funds to not only supplement certain sports/activities, but, in many cases, to help ensure their survival. While there are ethical issues related to fundraising among booster clubs that are beyond the scope of this chapter, it is important to mention them. Therefore, as a leader of the athletic programs, the athletic administrator(s) must be well educated and alert liaisons who communicate well with the booster club. Ultimately they must ensure that the role of the club is to *support* the athletic program and not determine *spending decisions/priorities* for the athletic program. Most booster clubs at the youth and interscholastic level are organized and administered by parents of the children in the youth sport, parents of student athletes in the school and at the intercollegiate level; many booster clubs are run and organized by supporters and fans of specific sports and activities. Simultaneously, many booster clubs at these levels are organized in a variety of ways, and as such, the point of this section of the chapter is twofold. The first aim of this chapter is to depict a *fundamental* organizational hierarchy that is mutual among the majority of youth, interscholastic and intercollegiate athletic programs across the United States. The second aim is to emphasize the importance of proper oversight that is initiated by the athletic administrator(s).

Booster clubs come in a variety of shapes and sizes; however, the fundamental element that defines their eventual success is measured in the amount of money that is contributed to the associated sports team or teams they are supporting. In the past, a popular way for booster clubs to raise money was in the sale of popcorn, hot dogs, candy and other food items held at the sporting event. Other fundraising activities included, but were not limited to, raffles and the sale of clothing and/or merchandise displaying the school's name and mascot. In many ways, this depicts the fundraising activities of the majority of interscholastic athletic programs in the United States over the past fifty years. However, as previously discussed, when we entered into the new millennium, the United States transitioned into the *age of technology*. As a result, this has had a significant impact on sports programs at all levels and dramatically altered the fundraising activities of booster clubs.

While the booster club organizational structure has remained fairly consistent in terms of title and description as sport programs have evolved over the last fifty years, the fundraising activities have experienced an increase in scope.

BOOSTER CLUB ORGANIZATIONAL HIERARCHY

In the United States, many booster clubs are organized in a variety of ways and with that in mind, the following is a generalized portrayal and description. For the most part, there are generally *three membership levels* of interscholastic athletic booster clubs that can include, but are not limited to the following: 1) Officers, 2) School Representatives, and 3) Committees (both standing and non-standing). Officers of the booster clubs can include the president, vice president, secretary and treasurer. These *officer* positions are generally elected on an annual basis. The role of the *president* is to provide general supervision of all athletic booster club meetings when they are present. Other duties of the president can include, but are not limited to, acting as responsible and effective stewards of the constitution, by-laws and rules of the booster club and acting as the designated representative to meet on a regular basis with the school representatives and other booster club officers.

The *vice president's* duties are usually intended to ensure that they are delegated to carry out the duties and responsibilities of the president in the event of the president's absence. Moreover, they are also responsible and effective stewards of the constitution, by-laws and rules of the booster club.

The role of the *secretary* is to be responsible for accurate recording of the dealings and meeting minutes of the athletic booster club. Other duties can include: maintaining attendance records of the membership; managing all mail and e-mail correspondence on behalf of the athletic booster club as well as to turn over all records, documentation, supplies and any other related equipment in their possession to their successor once their term as secretary has expired.

The role of the *treasurer* is to be the authorized custodian of all revenues of the athletic booster club and to deposit them in the club's accounts at a financial institution sanctioned by all three membership levels. The duties of the treasurer can include, but are not limited to: maintain an accurate and detailed account of all monies received and disbursed; reconcile all debts and bank statements and to resolve any discrepancies with the bank directly; if operating as a 501(c) (3) non-profit organization, to be the representative agent who files the annual IRS forms in a timely manner; and upon expiration of their term, they are to turn over all finances, records, balance sheets and other associated documentation to their successor, after a thorough audit by a neutral third-party auditor.

The role of *committees* is what differentiates interscholastic and intercollegiate booster clubs. The overall size and scope of the committees may differ, as may the type of work they are to accomplish. For instance, most booster clubs have *membership committees*, and they work, for the most part, to recruit and sign up new members as well as update the membership roster on a continual basis. Some membership committees may have a core group of five to ten people, some may have many more and others may have less than five.

Simultaneously, the membership committee may have a chairperson and a vice chair, whereas others don't. Many athletic booster club organizations have *standing and non-standing committees*, others do not. Some committees primarily function in the areas of communication, capital improvements, fundraising, concessions and merchandising. In many cases, *website development* is growing at a rapid pace among booster clubs in the United States. To clarify, standing committees are formed to do their assigned work on a continuous basis. Non-standing committees are, for the most part, dissolved once the task has been completed.

For example, the *Fundraising Committee* would be considered as a standing committee while the *Girls Basketball Hawaii Trip Committee* would be considered a non-standing committee or in some cases, referred to as an *ad hoc committee* because the particular committee was formed for a specific objective and ultimately terminated once the objective has been met. In many instances among athletic booster clubs across the United States, what *motivates* an individual to join and participate as an officer or standing or non-standing committee member has no singular answer. Some get involved because their children are involved as student athletes, while other participants like giving back to the school/community. A more thorough explanation will be devoted to Chapter 6 relative to the *fringe benefits* of booster clubs and the concept of *quid pro quo* among interscholastic athletic programs.

One of the essential aims of the booster club organization is to support all sport teams and programs by way of advocating fundraising and special events, fostering public relations and fan interest, as well as enhancing the school spirit through positive role modeling, promoting good sportsmanship and overall moral support. There are many cases across the United States among interscholastic athletic programs where the essential aims of the booster club organization are not unified. In many cases, there are separate booster clubs for the football team(s), basketball team(s), the marching band, etc. With this type of organizational orientation, it can become inefficient as well as lead to animosity among and between booster clubs. Furthermore, while certain stakeholders may cite that from a historical/traditional perspective, having separate clubs is the way things have been done, diplomatically working towards and implementing a uniform as well as unified booster club is ultimately the *best practice* for reinforcing the mission, goals and objectives which, in the long-term, benefits all stakeholders. Therefore, it may take years before a uniform/unified booster club can be fully integrated; however, the benefits far outweigh the drawbacks.

THE IMPORTANCE OF PROPER OVERSIGHT

Finally, if the athletic director completely understands the constitution, by-laws and rules from a technical standpoint, coupled with an appreciation of the importance of positive working relationships with the booster club members from a human relations standpoint in a unified environment, then success can be achieved. It should be clearly understood that the Director of Athletics is responsible in determining the *financial expenditures* for the athletic program, not the boosters. It is highly inappropriate for booster club members to concern themselves with the essential job functions of the athletic director. However, when individuals, such as boosters, who expend a significant amount of time and energy raising the funds to support the athletic program start to overstep their boundaries and start discussions that can *influence* the hiring and firing of certain personnel, it is up to the Director of Athletics to step in and discourage any communication that may detract the boosters from their objectives.

Nevertheless, proper *administrative oversight* of athletic booster clubs is essential to athletic program reputation and survival. Ultimately, it is through the proactive orientation of the Director of Athletics who must act in providing the necessary supervision. All too often throughout the United States, there are booster clubs in existence that have no formal constitution, by-laws or rules governing their organization. As a result, *booster club embezzlement* is a crime that has escalated in the United States (Popke 2008). There are numerous examples and cases of fraud due to lack of oversight. The North American Booster Club Association or NABCA, state that of the estimated 1.3 million booster clubs that support schools, colleges, universities, municipalities and private organizations, only a few of these booster clubs truly take the time that is necessary to develop by-laws and objectives (Popke 2008).

For example, a former high school sports booster club treasurer near Flint, Michigan embezzled approximately $48,000 from the account over a twelve-month period and the police investigators found $31,000 of it in cash at her home (Popke 2008). In Dallas, Texas at Bishop Lynch High School a former school employee who "handled cash proceeds from ticket sales at games and other events was indicted on felony theft charges in connection with more than $95,000 missing from the school's booster club coffers. School officials say she wrote checks to herself and forged the athletic director's signature" (Popke 2008, p.1).

At the intercollegiate level, the NCAA closely monitors the activities of booster clubs and has strict rules that are beyond the scope of this chapter to document. However, it must be noted and explained that over the years, the NCAA has investigated many scandals that have exposed activities by boosters among many intercollegiate athletic programs. As a result, in the majority of cases regarding intercollegiate booster clubs, improper monetary as well as in-kind incentives for prospective student athletes to sign with/attend a specific school were revealed by the NCAA. For instance, the NCAA uncovered a booster who was embezzling funds in excess of $1.2 million from her former employer to help fund trips and gifts for potential recruits at the University of Notre Dame (Litsky 1999).

Moreover, fraud, embezzlement and unethical behavior can be a double-edged sword, even among intercollegiate athletic administrations. In Memphis, Tennessee, a former University of Memphis assistant athletic director was found guilty and confessed to the embezzlement of approximately $75,000 as he victimized donors into believing they were writing checks to support the University of Memphis Tigers Club (Scruggs 2004). In most cases, they were instructed to write checks to phony marketing agencies which he had created. As a result, he convinced the donors that the University owed these false agencies money and embezzled it for his own personal use, but was ultimately caught after an internal audit of the financial records was completed (Scruggs 2004).

Among youth sport organizations, the opportunity for this type of fraud is escalating and stories appearing in the media are all too frequent. Theoretically, youth sports are ideally intended to help children learn valuable lessons about individual responsibility, integrity and teamwork. Moreover, developing a child's physical, emotional and social well-being are the desired outcomes of youth sport participation. On the other hand, as was mentioned in Chapter 1, the organizational structure of most youth sport organizations lacks administrative leadership, control and accountability. The lack of accountability is a key element for embezzlement due to the notion that many volunteer-run youth booster groups in the United States have no formal oversight by any organization just their own volunteers. In Paulo David's book, *Human Rights in Sports: A Critical Review of Children's Rights in Competitive Sports*, he comments on the lack of accountability concept by stating:

> Sports organizations have an obligation to protect the rights of young athletes, especially when one of their employees acts unlawfully. They cannot escape their responsibilities by failing to prevent violations or refusing to act upon them. But in practice, due to the tradition of self-policing, paternalism, a fierce resistance to independent criticism and a refusal to accept that sport is not always 'pure' and free from society's problems, the principles of accountability and scrutiny are still inadequately respected by the sporting world, or at best looked upon with suspicion.
>
> (David, P. in DeLench n.d., p.1)

Therefore, in the wake of such a harsh reality, fraudulent accounting practices and misappropriation of funds among youth, high school and intercollegiate athletic booster club organizations create awkward public relations situations for community youth sport organizations, school districts and/or colleges as a whole. Furthermore, a significant factor to keep in mind is the political backlash from the constituency if the institution(s) fail to take an active role in recovering or reimbursing the embezzled money. Finally, winning back the trust of the community in which the program exists can take a long time.

GENDER EQUITY

Books, articles, dissertations and case studies regarding Title IX and the issues of gender equity are abundant. To that end, it may appear that devoting a brief section in one part of the book is undervaluing its importance, quite the contrary. The fact is, so much has been written about the issues involving gender equity and Title IX that as a result of its voluminous magnitude, academics and practitioners alike are becoming increasingly desensitized to them (Gerdy 2000). Furthermore, it must be noted that there are excellent books, empirical research studies and other resources that sufficiently inform and evaluate gender equity from the perspective of fundraising and to that end, a list of resources will be presented at the end of this chapter for further review.

As leaders of youth, high school or even college athletic programs, there needs to be an understanding and appreciation of *integrating the tasks of doing things right with the commitment to do the right thing*. Administrative buzzwords such as *procedures, systematic operations* or *fundamental strategies* generally describe how to perform tasks and duties correctly. Undoubtedly, this is a very important piece of being organized, efficient and effective. Simultaneously, within the context of sports fundraising, being committed to creating a culture of compliance in regard to gender equity and Title IX is just as important.

"Making equitable efforts at fundraising or procuring sponsors for women's and men's teams ... demonstrates another example of the commitment toward the goal of gender equity as well" (Lyras and Hums 2009, p.8). However, in practice, primarily at the college level, these two objectives in many instances are unrealized as more emphasis is placed on the tasks of doing things right. As a result, failure to do the right thing has caused many college and university athletic departments to pay for expensive lawsuits due to Title IX violations.

Title IX compliance at the collegiate level has focused on issues to "evaluate collegiate athletic departments in their efforts to comply with Title IX. Equitable facilities travel and competition schedules, for example, would be signs of equal status" (Lyras and Hums 2009, p.8). A significant component beyond providing equitable allocation of resources relative to fundraising among booster clubs, Title

IX requires that women's and men's teams have *equitable benefits and service* regardless of where the source of money originates. For instance, if a high school or university athletic department accepts funds from an outside constituency such as a booster club or parent support group and gender differences are clearly obvious, those athletic departments could face Title IX charges. Similarly, Bonnette explains, "Where booster clubs provide benefits or services that assist only teams of one sex, the institution shall ensure that teams of the other sex receive equivalent benefits and services" (1990, p.5). In other words, if the men's basketball team receives new warm-up gear, then those items must be made available to the women's basketball team. Consequently, "Although single sport booster clubs are not forbidden, booster club monies do count in the Title IX equation. Research indicates that individual sport booster clubs play a major role in sport inequities and have contributed to the increase in the number of Title IX lawsuits seen across the country" (Prevosto 2009, p.9).

In conclusion, there are a variety of challenges and issues relative to gender equity in sports that go well beyond the concept of fundraising. Issues include, but are not limited to, participation opportunities for girls and women, scholarship monies, salaries for female coaches, and the lack of females in leadership positions like coach or athletic director. It's all about *balance* and to be a successful sport organization, the benefits of balance cannot be underestimated. Darlene Bailey, a leader in college athletic administration, summarizes this point best when she states:

> Despite what some may think, calls for gender equity do not mean the downfall of sport as we know it. It does not mean that men must be replaced as administrators and coaches. Rather it means that athletics will be far better off, far stronger and a much more viable component of the educational system, if we encourage feminine styles of leadership to balance the existing masculine styles. Just like our basketball team, men and women have to 'share the rock' if we expect athletics to come out a winner.
>
> (Bailey in J. R. Gerdy (ed) 2000, p.113)

Thus, it is important not only to *integrate the task of doing things right with the commitment to do the right thing*, but to also proactively embrace the concept that women have unique perspectives and experiences in addressing many issues in sports in general, including fundraising.

FURTHER READING

Bonnette, V. M. and Daniel, L. (1990) "Title IX Athletics Investigator's Manual", *ERIC Digest*, available at http://www.eric.ed.gov/PDFS/ED400763.pdf (accessed 01/31/12).

Brake, D. L. (2010) *Getting into the game: Title IX and the women's sports revolution*, New York: New York University Press.

Cook, R. (2011) "Process of adding a NCAA division I women's gymnastics program: A case study", University of Arkansas, available at http://search.proquest.com/docview/869739831?accountid=2909 (accessed 01/31/12).

Culbertson, B. K. (2008) "Supplementing annual school district budgets: Partnerships, fundraisers, foundations, and local support venues", University of North Texas, available at http://search.proquest.com/docview/304537768?accountid=2909 (accessed 01/31/12).

Frank, T. (2010) "Exploring the multiple roles of the modern national collegiate athletic association football bowl subdivision athletic director", Webster University, available at http://search.proquest.com/docview/822411064?accountid=2909 (accessed 01/31/12).

Gavora, J. (2002) *Tilting the Playing Field: School, Sports, Sex and Title IX*, San Francisco, CA: Encounter Books.

Gerdy, J. R. (2000) *Sports in school: The future of an institution*, New York: Teachers College Press.

Hardy, L. (2011) "Balancing the Booster Clubs", *American School Board Journal*, available at http://www.asbj.com/MainMenuCategory/Archive/2011/August/Balancing-the-Booster-Clubs.html (accessed 01/31/12).

Lyras, A. and Hums, M. A. (2009) "Sport and social change: The case for gender equality", *Journal of Physical Education, Recreation & Dance*, 80 (1) 7–8, 21, available at http://search.proquest.com/docview/215755394?accountid=2909 (accessed at 01/31/12).

McCartney, J. A. (2007) "The underrepresentation of women in athletics leadership: A qualitative study of NCAA division II women coaches and administrators", Capella University, available at

http://search.proquest.com/docview/304722742?accountid=2909 (accessed 01/31/12).
Meek, F. W. (2011) "Is your program at risk of being embezzled?" available at http://www.nays.org/CMSContent/File/For_administrators_-.pdf (accessed 01/31/12).
Reisch, J. T. and Seese, L. P. (2005) "Compliance with Title IX at Kingston State University: A case study on cost allocation and ethical decision making", *Issues in Accounting Education*, 20 (1) 81–97, available at http://search.proquest.com/docview/210916203?accountid=2909 (accessed 01/31/12).
Richie, C. S. (2004) "Georgia High School athletic directors' perceptions toward Title IX compliance in the state of Georgia", The University of Southern Mississippi, available at http://search.proquest.com/docview/305126721?accountid=2909 (accessed 01/31/12).
Selbe, D. S. (1997) "A comparison of high school principals' and athletic booster club presidents' perceptions of the role of football booster organizations in fundraising, governance issues, and personnel decisions", University of Southern California, available at http://search.proquest.com/docview/304369266?accountid=2909 (accessed 01/31/12).
Teel, K. A. (2005) "A study of the female athletic directors at NCAA division I and division II institutions", Baylor University, available at http://search.proquest.com/docview/305027165?accountid=2909 (accessed 01/31/12).

APPLICATION/SKILL BUILDING EXERCISE

Exercise 1: for students

Select a high school *and* a college/university of your choice to examine/study. Make an effort to contact the Director of Athletics at that particular school and college/university. Set up a face-to-face interview or perhaps a phone interview based on the availability/schedule of the Director of Athletics. Based on the chapter lesson regarding booster clubs, engage the Director of Athletics to answer the following six questions listed below. Additionally, *create* six distinctive questions of your own based on *your comprehension and interest* in the subject.

Document their responses relative to their experience and knowledge about:

- The athletic director's perception as to the reasons *why* there is a real need for booster clubs.
- The athletic director's perception as to the importance of recruiting and supervising coaches and the costs associated with hiring high-caliber personnel.
- The athletic director's perception of the skill sets necessary to work effectively with boosters.
- The athletic director's perception of professional ethics and administrative oversight of booster clubs.
- The athletic director's perception of a singular booster club compared to a multiple booster club structure.
- The athletic director's perception as to the importance of gender equity and Title IX compliance when accepting and spending booster club monies.

Exercise 2: for practitioners

Based on the chapter lesson regarding the need for booster clubs and Title IX compliance, attempt to thoroughly and honestly answer the following questions relative to your experience at your particular institution.

- Make an attempt to determine the following. How much does it cost to recruit and hire a new coach? (This can include things such as classified advertising costs, screening resumes, phone time costs to set appointments, interviewing costs, mail correspondence costs for thank-you letters and rejection letters, just to name a few).
- What skill sets have you found successful in working effectively with boosters and what areas can you identify that need improvement?
- How is your booster club organized in terms of structure? Is it a singular or multiple club structure?
- Who has the overall responsibility regarding administrative oversight of the booster(s) organization? Who does the booster club president report to? (The athletic director? The Building Principal? The Superintendent of Schools?)

Make an attempt to obtain the numbers and then think about the following question: how would you characterize the gender ratio of your school populations compared to the gender ratio of male and female athletes in your athletic program? How does the money from the booster club(s) then get distributed? How would you determine if your booster organization is in compliance with Title IX law?

CHAPTER 3

PERSONAL SKILL SET DEVELOPMENT IN FUNDRAISING

The intent of this chapter is to identify and explain the personal skill sets essential in athletic fundraising. Personal characteristics and skill acquisition strategies will be addressed as well as contemporary issues and practical applications at the youth, interscholastic and intercollegiate levels.

PERSONAL CHARACTERISTICS

In administering an athletic program at either the interscholastic or intercollegiate levels, the personal skill sets that would aid in developing an individual in the fundraising arena include, but are not limited to, the following five characteristics:

- interpersonal competency skills
- efficient managerial and teaching skills
- perseverance skills
- self-image skills
- ethical skills.

Interpersonal competency skills are skill sets that an individual must develop in order to be an effective athletic fundraiser. Also referred to as *people skills*, athletic administrators wear many hats and are responsible to many stakeholders of the athletic program in the school and the community at large. In rallying support, especially in raising funds for athletics, an individual must be a good listener and composed when dealing with anyone. People must feel that their inquiries, demands and/or needs are being addressed. Today's athletic fundraiser is a diplomatic spokesperson for the merits of the athletic program and must realize that everyone is important. People skills are vitally important when the athletic fundraiser wants to promote his/her athletic program and champion goodwill. The essence of directing athletics is communicating and having the necessary interpersonal skills to know when to pursue, when to back off and listen, when to be aggressive, and much more.

As mentioned in Chapter 1, whether it is due to the changing career path or the disposable income of a donor, the declining economy or perhaps an over-saturation of charitable and worthwhile causes in the marketplace, raising funds is a challenging endeavor. Contemporary athletic fundraisers need to be comfortable with rejection and be able to deal with it when it occurs, because rejection will happen. In order to gain support from people of divergent backgrounds and interests, the athletic fundraiser must discover what desires, goals, objectives and needs they have in common. Your ability to influence people will depend largely on how effective you are at discovering the tie that binds. This is why interpersonal competency skills are so critical. Therefore, you must listen, take advice, lose arguments and in many cases, follow. You must realize that in leading an athletic fundraising initiative, you're not going to have all of the answers and furthermore, you can't do it alone.

In order to enhance your people skills, you must be flexible enough to receive input from the various constituencies by getting out and listening to their perspective. This approach goes a long way toward solving problems arising from community interests that demand winning teams regardless of policies and goals designed to promote the best educational development for student athletes. That is why people skills are so fundamentally important in properly administering athletic programs. Critics can be turned into stakeholders. Once stakeholders of the athletic program feel that they have been heard, they will follow your lead. Taken as a whole, this will help you in the long term as a relationship-builder for your athletic program. Being committed to improving your people skills will aid in making you more successful as an athletic fundraiser.

Efficient managerial and teaching skills are skill sets that involve intelligent action. As detailed in Chapter 1, once the fundraising *prerequisites* (mission, goals and objectives) have been clearly articulated and implemented, action must happen in a practical, productive and competent fashion. This is what's referred to as *efficiency*. From a mathematical/scientific perspective, calculating efficiency is equal to outputs divided by inputs. However, when approaching a fundraising initiative for an athletic program, that calculation is too simplistic. Efficiency is ultimately about choosing the best strategy to accomplish the goals. Efficiency also involves hiring and managing competent staff or volunteer workers and being accountable. A significant reality among many interscholastic athletic programs in the United States is that the support for their programs is fragmented. As mentioned in Chapter 2, a significant element to fundraising is having a single, *unified* booster club whose essential aim is to support all sport teams and programs. Having one cohesive club benefits all stakeholders of the school and community at large because fundraising efforts are carried out in a coordinated fashion.

An additional *prerequisite* involves crafting and teaching the merits of the mission. It is a mutual process of uniting stakeholders in conversations about their hopes, aspirations and dreams and in due course, aiding to provide the fundamental rationale for supporting the athletic program. Simply put, you have to teach the mission for the program to the people in your athletic booster club and community. Especially when it comes to fundraising initiatives, contemporary athletic leadership is about exchanging ideas. Contemporary athletic leadership isn't about imposing the athletic director's sole philosophy; it's about developing a shared sense of destiny. It's about enlisting others to communicate so that they can contribute their interests and aspirations that are aligned with the mission and as such, can commit to activate their individual talents toward its achievement.

Efficiency in athletic fundraising not only involves getting stakeholders aligned with the mission of the athletic department, it also involves meticulous record-keeping of fundraising activities that not only were *successful*, but also those fundraising activities that failed. From an efficiency standpoint, keeping accurate records of the specific details allows for *replication* of the successful fundraisers and simultaneously, those that did not yield much money can be reevaluated or discontinued. In sum, when it comes to raising money for the athletic department, being efficient includes the cost-effectiveness of expenditure on the fundraising activities as well as the personnel and time costs.

Perseverance skills are skill sets that involve the mindset of never quitting. Perseverance involves hard work, commitment, patience, and endurance. Perseverance is being able to overcome obstacles calmly and without complaint. In athletic fundraising, applying this skill is essential to fundraising success. Whether it is cultivating a prospective donor, attempting to close a corporate sponsorship, or writing a grant proposal, in all of these instances, we are in a position of power and control. Perseverance requires *attentional focus* and therefore, a sports fundraiser needs to disregard the things that are outside of their control (chance, external circumstances, the economy, etc.) and ultimately concentrate on the things they can control, which will eventually produce desirable results. Jimmy Valvano, former basketball coach and Director of Athletics at N.C. State University in Raleigh, North Carolina and television broadcaster, battled cancer and in his ESPY Awards speech on 4 March 1993, he introduced the motto "Don't give up, don't ever give up" (The V Foundation 2010, p.1). Based on the speech that he gave, the motto of his V Foundation is the *epitome of perseverance.*

So, in your position as a sports fundraiser, when circumstances or the task at hand is difficult, perseverance is the capacity to keep working toward the objective and is the *skill* to remain steadfast at a difficult task.

Self-image skills are skill sets that involve dual elements of one's actions and their personal presence. Also referred to as *self-concept*, it is the mental image one has of oneself. Much of how an individual's self-image is developed is by personal experiences and the internalization of judgments made by others. When it comes to sports fundraising, donors need to *entrust* that their hard-earned money will be used appropriately for the intended purposes. As a result, a sport fundraiser needs to be a diplomatic spokesperson for the merits of the athletic program and they must present themselves to the public at large with the utmost professionalism. The old metaphorical phrase, "don't judge a book by its cover", means that individuals should not make up their mind about a certain thing based on its appearance. Regardless of how one interprets the phrase, many people in our society do tend to judge people and circumstances based on appearance. When it comes to raising funds for sports programs, having the most positive and professional presence is a key element. Therefore, questions generally will gravitate towards does the Director of Athletics at XYZ University speak well in public? Is the clothing they wear clean and neat in appearance? Are they well groomed? Do they have any annoying habits? Ultimately, the image we project to the public can have a significant impact, fair or unfair, on how the funds for the athletic program are secured. Therefore, it is imperative that a sports fundraiser undertake careful analysis of things such as clothing, personal grooming, speech and mannerisms as well as other personal characteristics and actions.

Projecting a positive self-image to the various stakeholders of the athletic program is a very significant component to fundraising. A notable example of a person who depicts *self-image skills* is Gene Smith, Director of Athletics at the Ohio State University. There, Smith oversees one of the nation's largest and most successful college athletic programs. The Buckeyes have thirty-six fully-funded varsity sports and more than 1,000 student athletes. The department of athletics is completely self-supporting and receives no university funds, tax dollars or student fees. In fiscal year 2008–9, the department transferred nearly $26 million in assessments to the university, including more than $13 million in grant-in-aid reimbursement. In Smith's first three years at Ohio State, the department of athletics finished in the black financially and increased its reserve fund (Gene Smith Biography 2010). Overall, success in fundraising requires careful analysis of *oneself* and how one projects professionalism in a diplomatic fashion, when times are good as well as when times are bad.

Ethical and integrity skills are skill sets that essentially guide an individual to do the right thing from an external system of rules and norms that valuates right and wrong, combined with being honest and forthright with themselves both personally and professionally. As stated in Chapter 2, there have been significant cases where a lack of ethics and integrity caused people in leadership roles at both the interscholastic and intercollegiate athletic fundraising levels to act mischievously, by embezzling funds intended for the betterment of the sport program and student athletes. All too often, the actions of a few can cause irreparable harm to the athletic program, the school and the community, which can take many years to overcome.

There are a broad spectrum of issues relative to ethics and integrity in sports fundraising, yet, there are three significant issues within sports fundraising that should be acknowledged that include, but are not limited to, the following:

- High-pressure sales techniques: instances such as telephone solicitations, postal mail solicitations, e-mail solicitations, and face-to-face solicitations where the solicitor refuses to take no for an answer. If this is a fundraising tactic or practice used by your sport organization where making high-pressure solicitations is the norm, the supporters of the athletic program may question the credibility of the organization. Credibility is the ultimate basis of leading any interscholastic or intercollegiate athletic program and it can be significantly diminished by an overzealous selling technique. As a rule of thumb, there is no place for aggressive/high-pressure solicitation in sports fundraising.
- Augmenting financial data: generally referred to in the accounting world as *cooking the books*, or *creative accounting*. Overall, augmenting financial data is the unethical falsifying of finances to mislead others into thinking that the financial status of the organization is either better off, or perhaps worse off, than it really is. For example, a booster club may look into luring new investors/donors or perhaps get a bank loan for a specific fundraising project such as a new press box, new weightlifting equipment or even a new artificial sports surface. Consequently, the booster club may augment the financial statements so that they *appear* to have more money than they actually have. This is a tactic to boost the confidence of the prospective investors/donors or the lending institution. Not only is this kind of tactic unethical, it is also illegal and punishable by law. In most cases, after an independent audit, most sport organizations who utilize this unethical practice get caught. Conversely, some try the tactic of falsifying their financial statements to give the appearance that they have *less money* than they actually have in order to get grants and/or government aid. Overall, this is exactly where the administrative oversight of the Director of Athletics and the use of a third-party independent auditor are needed, so that unethical financial accounting practices are discouraged at all levels.
- Misleading donors/stakeholders: a situation where the donor/stakeholder is told that their money is being used for the intended purpose but is in fact being used for something else. While this occurs primarily among intercollegiate athletics, the number of cases at the youth and interscholastic levels is rising. For example, the athletic department at XYZ University might state that the money that was donated is to be used for *X*, but the athletic

administration might take the money and apply it to *Y*. Therefore, does the administration modify what the money was intended for? That is certainly unethical, yet it happens fairly often. This is a clear example of where things can get muddled and result in a *gray area*.

In general, gifts of many sizes and amounts come with strings attached. Large, significant gifts always come with strings attached and it is very unusual for the athletic department to be given $500,000 and be told, "I trust you and support you to use it however you want". As a result, the donors will specify that they want the money to go to the Basketball Program or the Football Program or perhaps the Student Athlete Academic Advising Department. Consequently, it is incumbent upon the athletic department to use the money in which the donor said they wanted it to go towards. Being responsible and allocating the gifted money toward the area(s) in which the donor has indicated is all part of *stewarding the gift*, which will be explained in greater detail in Chapter 5. In essence, stewarding the gift means that the athletic department, as the steward, is "being responsible for something valuable on behalf of someone who has entrusted it to our care" (Conway 2003, p.432).

The misleading of donors by not honoring the intent of their donation is not only unethical, but in the end, will erode trust. Generally, a college and/or university athletic department's aim is not only to attract new donors, but ultimately *maintain* them. In sum, learning the proper skills of stewardship is essential. Whether it is through the use of annual or semi-annual financial data reports, simple acts of appreciation and acknowledgement, or careful accounting procedures, being genuine and accountable are essential skill sets to possess in contemporary athletic fundraising.

SKILL ACQUISITION

Important to the overall development of a sports fundraiser are the opportunities that exist to perform/practice the skills that were learned through various situations such as formal classroom instruction, readings, application exercises, etc. *Skill acquisition* in sports fundraising can include, but is not limited to, internships, volunteer opportunities at the interscholastic level, volunteer opportunities at the intercollegiate level, as well as volunteer opportunities within the non-profit sector. While the lessons learned in the classroom need to be based on sound theory and delivered in a professional manner, the *internship* is a key component to the development of the sports fundraiser.

Historically, the concept of the internship has its roots from the introduction of cooperative education, commonly referred to as *co-op education*. The Co-op was founded on 24 September 1906 by Herman Schneider, a University of Cincinnati Professor of Civil Engineering (Riley 2006). In particular, the "Co-op is the practice wherein students regularly alternate time spent in the classroom with time spent in the workforce as paid professionals" (Riley 2006, p.12). Co-op education had its cynics back in the early 1900s just as the field of sport administration/sport management had its share of controversy associated with curriculum development, which will be detailed further in Chapter 10.

Accordingly, "Sport, and to a greater degree, the management of sport organizations, is so unique and so unusual, that the debates, problems and growing pains associated with curriculum development reflect its versatility" (Kelley 2002, p.30). In fact, many research studies in the area of curriculum development in sport administration/sport management conducted in the late 1980s and early 1990s identified the field experience/internship as a necessary element in preparing students majoring in sport management. Stier explains, "The internship experience is a critical part of the formal education of any future sport manager" (1999, p.46).

As time progressed and the field of sport management was formally recognized as a legitimate area of study, the National Association for Sport and Physical Education (NASPE) joined forces with the North American Society for Sport Management (NASSM) and in 1993, created the NASPE-NASSM Program Standards that outline the minimum core content for undergraduate and graduate programs in sport management (Kelley 2002). Between 1993 and 1999, the Sport Management Program Review Council (SMPRC) was developed and is the supervisory body that maintains standards of excellence in undergraduate and graduate education for sport management (Kelley 2002). Overall, the SMPRC requires that sport management programs must have their undergraduate students engage in a field experience. As for master's and doctoral students, the SMPRC does have requirements that are modified, taking into consideration that most master's and doctoral level students already have experience working in the sport management field.

PRACTICAL APPLICATIONS

In addition to internship experience, there is significant value in volunteering one's time at either the interscholastic or intercollegiate levels. In fact, a large percentage of interscholastic athletic programs across the United States are in need of volunteers for their fundraising initiatives. This can be a valuable experience for those entering the profession and the benefits are threefold:

- Direct involvement with the community: a great opportunity to give back and get involved with the school and community athletic fundraiser. By being involved in helping raise funds for the success of the school's athletic program, this type of participation draws people in and strengthens the sense of community and of belonging as you promote school and team spirit and support the program. It also helps as a resume builder and shows potential sport organizations that you are driven, dedicated and have a strong work ethic.
- Learn new skills: you can learn to develop customer service telephone and/or interpersonal skills, spreadsheet application skills, sales skills, leadership skills as well as others to broaden your horizons. Ultimately, volunteering for a sports fundraiser and developing new skills that could potentially be beneficial to your career. You may reveal interests you were unaware of, become motivated to learn more about an aspect of sports fundraising that appeals to you, or you may decide that sports fundraising is not for you and as such, you may choose a new career path.
- Broadens social networking opportunities/builds lifelong friendships: social networking is a valuable tool to increasing your prospects of making new contacts as well as the potential it has in advancing one's career. An acquaintance could eventually turn out to be the key to a new career opportunity. Remember, a sports fundraising group activity is the perfect setting in which to

impress those stakeholders of the athletic organization and show off your abilities. Moreover, by being around people who are like-minded and share a passion for sports, this is a great way to meet and build lifelong friendships as well.

In the sports fundraising landscape, as was mentioned previously in this chapter, today's athletic fundraiser is a diplomatic spokesperson for the merits of the athletic program and must realize that everyone is important. Many interscholastic athletic programs in the United States have been burdened with deficit. Additionally, in some cases there is an ever increasing apathy among the general public concerning the importance placed on athletics in relation to the academic missions of schools. Combined with the financial challenges that were covered in Chapter 1 as well as the ethical issues referenced earlier among booster organizations, the prospect of leading an athletic program can be daunting.

Therefore, the major topic for consideration here is that if the personal skill sets in this book are taken seriously, this will certainly aid in the extreme need for *administrative reform* among youth, interscholastic and intercollegiate athletic programs throughout the United States. Part of this *reform* must come from the development of curriculum among undergraduate and graduate programs in Sport Administration/Sport Management. Furthermore, within the curriculum, those entering the sport management field at either the interscholastic or intercollegiate level need to not only learn lessons on how to successfully raise funds for athletics within the current economic context, but also learn from the mistakes of the past. This will ultimately aid in gaining a well-balanced perspective so that one can be better equipped to handle the everyday tasks in an ethical and professional manner. More specific and detailed information regarding curriculum development will be presented in Chapter 10. Optimistically, the ethical commitment of athletic administrators, both current and future, to seek out new revenue streams and manage clear fundraising initiatives as a "means to improve the financial stability of their athletic programs will translate into significant benefits for their most important investment, the student athletes" (Kelley 2000, p.51).

FURTHER READING

Barna, P. J. (2009) "Ethical behavior in the framework of educational and ethical leadership: Grounded theory research", University of Phoenix, available at http://search.proquest.com/docview/305124513?accountid=2909 (accessed 01/31/12).

Branch, D. (1990) "Athletic director leader behavior as a predictor of intercollegiate athletic organizational effectiveness", *Journal of Sport Management*, 2 (4) 161–173.

Christian, H. R. (2000) "Leadership styles and characteristics of athletic directors", University of Alabama, available at http://search.proquest.com/docview/304587707?accountid=2909 (accessed 01/31/12).

Cormier, J. (2008) "Multi-frame leadership, goal orientation their relationship to organizational effectiveness in intercollegiate athletics", University of New Mexico, available at http://search.proquest.com/docview/304525698?accountid=2909 (accessed 01/31/12).

Doherty, A. J. (1997) "The effect of leader characteristics on the perceived transformational/transactional leadership and impact of interuniversity athletic administrators", *Journal of Sport Management*, 11 (3) 275–285.

Gower, R. K. (2008) "Internships in recreation, sport and tourism: Exploring student perceptions", University of Illinois at Urbana-Champaign, available at http://search.proquest.com/docview/304604887?accountid=2909 (accessed 01/31/12).

Harrison, T. M. (2004) "Internal stakeholder perceptions of intercollegiate athletic reform: A focus group examination", The Ohio State University, available at http://search.proquest.com/docview/305139369?accountid=2909 (accessed 01/31/12).

Hylton, K. and Bramham, P. (eds) (2008) *Sports development: Policy, process and practice*, London: Routledge.

Loland, S. (2002) *Fair play in sport: A moral norm system*, London: Routledge.

Moriarty, E. (2000) "Hands-on experience key for students in VCU program", *SportsBusiness Journal*, available at http://www.sportsbusinessdaily.com/Journal/Issues/2000/12/20001211/No-Topic-Name.aspx (accessed 01/31/12).

Parkhouse, B. (1996) *The management of sport: Its foundations and application* (2nd edn), St. Louis: Mosby-Year Book.

Peng, H. (2000) "Competencies of sport event managers in the United States", University of Northern Colorado, available at http://search.proquest.com/docview/304612849?acccountid=2909 (accessed 01/31/12).

Spivey, L. M. (2008) "Division I athletics directors and university presidents: A comparison of sport-related values", available at http://search.proquest.com/docview/250809284?accountid=2909 (accessed 01/31/12).

Trail, G. and Chelladurai, P. (2002) "Perceptions of intercollegiate athletic goals and processes: The influence of personal values", *Journal of Sport Management*, 16 (4) 289–310.

Young Jr., J. F. (2009) "Texas rural public school superintendents' perceptions of the role of the high school athletic director", Sam Houston State University, available at http://search.proquest.com/docview/305066300?accountid=2909 (accessed 01/31/12).

APPLICATION/SKILL BUILDING EXERCISE

Exercise 1: for students

Select a youth sport, a high school, or a college/university athletic department of your choice to volunteer your time for a fundraising initiative. Research and determine who the key personnel are and reach out and contact them either by telephone, e-mail or make the effort to set up an appointment to meet face-to-face. Once you become involved as a volunteer for an athletic fundraiser, keep a journal from start to finish and compile your perceptions and feelings among the following areas:

- How did your participation with the athletic fundraiser enhance your direct involvement with the community?
- Identify and explain the new skills you learned as a volunteer (i.e. customer service telephone and/or interpersonal skills, spreadsheet application skills, sales skills, leadership skills, etc.) and how did this experience broaden your horizons?
- How did your participation with the athletic fundraiser broaden your social network? Did you make any new friendships? Did you

work with or meet anyone that could potentially be beneficial to your career? Could this experience lead to an internship opportunity?

- What were your overall perceptions and feelings about the fundraising experience in terms of strengths and weaknesses of the leadership provided? Can you identify and explain specific elements and/or procedures that you liked and/or would change to improve the experience?

Exercise 2: for practitioners

Select a fundraising activity that you were involved with either at the youth sport, high school, or college/university level. Reflect on the experience in terms of planning and organizing the activities as well as your work with volunteers, and compile your perceptions and feelings among the following areas:

- Based on a past athletic fundraiser, who was responsible in determining who was on the planning committee? Who was involved in helping choose the best strategies to accomplish the goals? How were volunteers recruited?
- What type of documentation and/or data collection was compiled and who was responsible for collecting the information? What were the procedures or criteria of determining whether or not the past fundraising activities were a success or not?
- How did your participation with the athletic fundraiser broaden your constituency? Did you work with or meet anyone that could help recruit new booster club members? Was there a businessperson from the private sector or a community business owner at your fundraiser who could be cultivated as a potential sponsor?

Based on the skills detailed in this chapter (interpersonal competency skills, efficient managerial and teaching skills, perseverance skills, self-image skills, and ethical skills) what were the general strengths and weaknesses of the leadership you provided? Can you identify and explain any specific procedures that you would change to improve the experience based on what you have learned in this chapter? For example, could you build your volunteer base to include college sport management students looking for practicum/internships?

CHAPTER 4

DYNAMIC FUNDRAISING ESSENTIALS AND PRINCIPLES

The intent of this chapter is to identify and explain the substantial principles and models in successful sports fundraising. There are distinct differences between the fundraising activities conducted at the college level compared to those at youth and high school levels. Nevertheless, despite these differences, there are fundamental principles, techniques, models, guidelines and challenges to effectively plan, communicate, implement and manage that are applicable at all levels. Another aim of this chapter is to cover basic fundraising fundamentals: *the Rosso LAI Principle, the fundraising cycle* and *the 90–10 Principle.*

Intercollegiate and youth and high school athletic fundraising activities have both unique elements and common elements. As stated in Chapter 1, one of the primary differences between fundraising at the intercollegiate level in comparison to youth and high school athletic programs is that they are more orientated toward ROI (*return on investment*) and philanthropy. Also, the size and scope of the organizations relative to both human and financial resources are another facet that differentiates intercollegiate and youth/interscholastic athletic programs. Figure 4.1 illustrates this concept visually; it shows that they have distinct features as well as common or shared elements at the intersection in the middle.

FUNDRAISING FUNDAMENTALS AND THE ROSSO LAI PRINCIPLE

When it comes to fundraising at either the intercollegiate or youth and/or high school athletic levels, there are a few basic fundamentals intended to guide and facilitate fundraising. The *fundraising prerequisites*

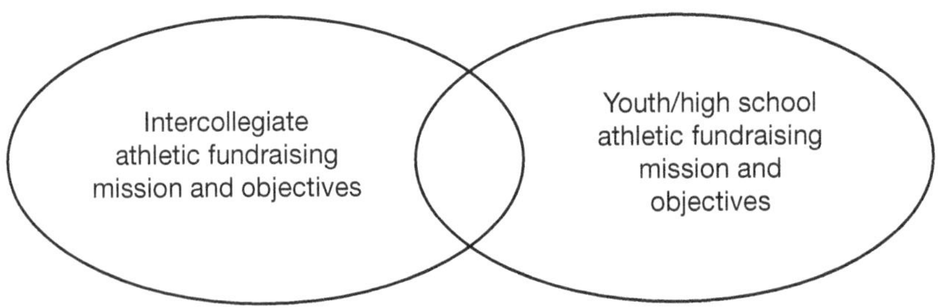

Figure 4.1 The Kelley Athletic Fundraising Diagram

detailed in Chapter 1 should preferably be accomplished before the fundraising activities commence. Within the conceptual framework of the prerequisites, the basic fundraising fundamentals that should be acknowledged include, but are not limited to, the following:

- planning and goal setting
- identifying and targeting the constituency
- rallying support and involvement
- organizing and managing time, money and resources
- evaluating the results.

Planning and Goal Setting

Various elements will come into play when fundraising for sports programs. Prioritizing what is needed is a key element. For example, is this a capital campaign that is aimed at raising enough money to build a new sport facility? Is this an initiative to raise enough to purchase and install a new multipurpose artificial grass field? Is this a fundraising campaign for a *special event*, to raise enough money so that the women's basketball team can travel and play in an overseas tournament in a foreign country? Is this a *general fundraiser* intended to help pay for uniforms and/or equipment? Whatever the reason, the Director of Athletics needs to provide *proactive leadership* in order to determine the priorities, through judicious communication of those initiatives/goals with the stakeholders/constituency. Once the fundraising initiative has been established, the *planning and goal setting* phase starts. It is from this phase of sports fundraising that the subsequent fundamental areas are projected.

Therefore, identifying/targeting the constituency, rallying support and involvement, anticipating the amount of time, money and resources as well as the type of evaluation tools to be used are all addressed and projected into a course of action. Fittingly, this is the time when the words, ideas and thoughts are documented and ultimately communicated to all stakeholders, volunteers and community members. The importance of the planning/goal setting phase cannot be overestimated. Individuals, if they are to be committed to your organization, must have the opportunity to be involved in this phase. Proper lead time must be provided as well. Not allowing an appropriate amount of time to involve prospects/stakeholders to help plan and set goals prior to your fundraising drive is ill-advised. Therefore, it is highly recommended to continuously *involve* prospects/stakeholders in the planning and goal setting phase so that they feel a sense of ownership and are ultimately committed to the initiative from conception to conclusion. Simultaneously, setting deadlines is an important part of the planning and goal setting phase. When there is too much deliberation and no enforced prescribed deadlines, this can lead to a *paralysis by analysis* situation. In sports fundraising, you need to be proactive and keep to a schedule with target dates that are communicated clearly and understood by all involved in the planning and goal setting phase.

Another significant piece of this phase is to set realistic goals. As covered in Chapter 1, goals should be SMART. SMART stands for *Specific*, *Measurable*, *Achievable*, *Results-oriented*, and *Time-determined* (Seiler 2003). Overall, it is within this phase where *who, what, where, when* and *why* are fully examined and documented and this becomes a *road map* that guides people's actions. Consequently, when fundraising goals are not determined at the outset and the prevailing attitude is *to raise as much money as possible*, this is when the project is most susceptible to fraud and embezzlement. Proper administrative oversight of this phase by the Director of Athletics will determine if the fundraising activities will be purposeful or aimless.

Identifying and Targeting the Constituency

Also referred to as defining the *stakeholders*, this is the part of the fundraising process that involves not only classifying people into internal and external groups, but also figuring out what motivates them to donate their money. *Alumni, parents, faculty, staff, past student athletes, booster club members, fans, past contributors, coaches, administrators, volunteers, businesses and corporations, news media,* and *service organizations* could all be considered as the constituency of the athletic program.

As explained in Chapter 1, the *constituency model* (Seiler 2003) provides an excellent visual representation of this phase of the fundraising process. As soon as the constituency is identified, then they need to be qualified by three criteria; this is known as the *Rosso LAI Principle.* Henry "Hank" Rosso is considered as the founding father of ethical and philanthropic fundraising. His philosophy has influenced thousands in the non-profit fundraising profession and despite his passing in 1999, his wisdom and teachings flourish. Additionally, Rosso's LAI Principle has also had a significant impact among intercollegiate athletic development professionals. In a conversation with Bob Arkeilpane, University of Cincinnati Deputy Director of Athletics, he commented that Rosso's LAI Principle is an important planning tool in terms of how the feasibility of athletic fundraising campaigns is tested and delivered at Cincinnati. Essentially, *linkage* refers to the human connection the prospect has with the organization, *ability* refers to the financial ability of the prospect to give gifts at the level being sought, and *interest* refers to the degree to which the prospect is interested in becoming involved with the organization (Maxwell 2003). For example, it is good fundraising practice to identify and then target prospective donors who display all three criteria.

The linkage may be that the prospect is not only an alumnus of the school, but is also a former student athlete. Simultaneously, of the three areas (linkage, ability and interest), ability is the least reliable indicator of charitable giving. However, ability must be considered based on the level of money being sought. The last indicator, interest, might be that the prospect is a season ticket holder and attends games on a regular basis.

Finally, if all three criteria are present and judicious time and effort are used to create mutually beneficial alliances between the constituency and the athletic program, fundraising success can be achieved. Moreover, a scoring system can be incorporated in order to *quantify* the prospects, which can help direct cultivation and solicitation energies toward those corporations or individuals who are most likely to supply financial backing. It makes no sense to target the individuals within a certain constituency who have the most money to give (ability) if there is no linkage or interest in the work of the athletic program. As a result, the effort to focus only on those individuals who have the greatest financial ability becomes a waste of time.

In terms of the scoring system, a basic rating scale can be applied. In the category of linkage, as previously mentioned, the individual has a connection with the sport organization. The following is a brief description of how to measure and/or quantify the linkage, ability and interest elements. For the purposes of this basic scoring example, one way of assessing the linkage is to rate the past giving behavior of the prospect and their relationship to the sport organization. Therefore a five-point rating system can be incorporated (Wylie 2004). A score of one is equal to infrequent or no record of giving; two is equal to a one-time gift; three is equal to an occasional or lapsed donor; four is equal to a frequent annual donor and a five is equal to a frequent major gift donor. Ability can be quantified among a range of money-giving levels among the five-point rating system.

Hypothetically, let's assume a score of one is equal to $0–$1,499; a score of two is equal to $1,500–$4,999; a score of three is equal to $5,000–$19,999; a score of four is equal to $20,000–$49,999 and a score of five is equal to $50,000–$100,000 or higher. Interest can be measured as the following:

- A score of one is equal to limited or no knowledge of the sport organization.
- A score of two is equal to minimal involvement with the sport organization, perhaps a one-time attendance at a sporting event.
- A score of three is equal to moderate interest in and/or occasional attendance at sporting events or limited involvement with the booster or fundraising activities.
- A score of four is equal to moderate involvement with the sport organization, frequently attending sporting events and or a connection with a booster club member/moderate involvement with fundraising activities.
- A score of five is equal to active involvement with the sport organization as a season ticket holder or active involvement as a booster member and/or volunteering for fundraising activities.

In general, the creation of such a rating system needs to be carefully and judiciously planned. The financial context of the sport organization will certainly determine the scale of the rating system. For instance, a score of two in the ability category for an intercollegiate athletic program could be more like a four for a youth sport program. Therefore, careful planning and analysis in the creation of these scales is of great importance. Once calibrated, the decision of whether to assess the overall rating system needs to be determined. An overall score of eleven out of fifteen for one sport organization may be *statistically* strong enough to qualify a prospect to the *cultivation* stage, whereas another sport organization may require thirteen out of fifteen. It should be noted at this point that whatever rating scale is used and the associated score, if it does not meet at least fifty percent or seven and a half out of fifteen, then the prospect or *lead* should not be in consideration for further cultivation.

Likewise, there needs to be a strategic starting point in rating and scoring prospects. As a result, once the prospect rating instrument is calibrated and the scoring system is assessed, it should yield reliable results.

Rallying Support and Involvement

Sports fundraising is a dynamic endeavor. It involves actively recruiting individuals to provide their valuable time, money and other resources toward the mission and objectives of the athletic program. One of the primary *conduits* of activating and/or rallying support and involvement is the student athletes themselves. This is based on the notion that since these athletes have direct contact with many other individuals, including their parents, they are able to convey the positive aspects of their sports experience (Stier 2001). Additionally, rallying support and involvement for fundraising involves focusing on the natural constituencies mentioned previously in this chapter.

In sum, when attempting to rally support and involvement from the community, there are three areas to consider. First is to *educate the stakeholders about the mission and goals of the sport organization.* As was detailed in Chapter 1, the effectiveness of a sport organization at identifying, cultivating and ultimately attracting people closer and closer to the center of Seiler's constituency model, and drawing them to its mission, will largely depend upon how well they *connect* and pay attention to the needs and values of the constituents. The less informed your constituents are about the mission and/or goals of the organization, the less they will want to get involved. Displaying a proactive, enthusiastic approach coupled with gathering significant facts and figures to present to supporters will go a long way if it can touch and/or move booster club members, students or others in the community personally. Second, is to *make sure that the fundraising goals are realistically attainable.* While this consideration appears obvious, when fundraising activities are initiated, it can raise the old idiom *biting off more than you can chew.* This type of situation can lead to frustration and could drive away volunteers in the process.

The final consideration is to *make it fun, enjoyable and express appreciation for volunteers and donors.* Volunteers and donors are often the best fundraisers and empowering them to seek additional supporters is a great way to grow sport organizations and further their missions. A key element is ensuring that they are appreciated, as this goes a long way toward fundraising success in both the short and long term. Moreover, focusing on actions of gratitude through personalized "thank-you" messages will ultimately make it easier to ask for money next time you need it. Therefore, the following three-pronged approach should be considered significant in rallying support and involvement from volunteers:

1 Organize a fundraising campaign kickoff party and a closing party that focuses on the positive work of the fundraiser.
2 Be open-minded to volunteer suggestions and give kudos to them on a constant and consistent basis.
3 Have a rewards system for the volunteers each time they reach a goal; this can be accomplished through the use of praise as well as public displays of appreciation.

In particular, be proactive in conveying your appreciation and recognition of donors, volunteers, supporters, and helpers within the sport organization and the community. Applying this type of orientation in connection with paying attention to the needs and values of the constituents will help draw them into the mission of the organization and support it financially.

Organizing and Managing Time, Money and Resources

Individuals in the intercollegiate athletic domain who are full-time *athletic development personnel* clearly have an advantage in this area compared to those in the interscholastic athletic domain, in terms of both human and financial resources. Irrespective of that difference, there are still the requisite organizational tasks of goal setting and prioritizing, processing paperwork, delegating effectively, eliminating time wasters, making fundraising meetings productive, and controlling procrastination while properly utilizing technology at both levels. When analyzing the prudent use of time, money and resources, athletic administrators, regardless of the level they are managing, need to acknowledge that *technology* and the utilization of *stakeholders* should guide their strategies. Much of the focus of this area will be in the identification and targeting of the constituency or *pool of prospects*. As a result, "You may have little control over who your constituents are, but you have tremendous control over how you spend your time and resources" (Birkholtz 2008, p.73). Furthermore, the use of technology will certainly aid in facilitating this process. In sports fundraising, the goal is to efficiently build a predictive modeling system that "will eventually help us pick out people in your database who are likely to give frequently (and hopefully in large quantity) to the university" (Wylie 2004, p.7).

Obvious *hard data* that is contained or housed in the computer database and/or spreadsheets of athletic development officers are *variables* that can include, but are not limited to, total giving history, annual income, net worth, total assets, contributions to other charitable organizations, etc. However, there are other *soft data* variables in most databases that are related to giving but are thus far untapped. Variables in most databases can include, but are not limited to, the following categories:

- Constituent Categories: includes groups such as alumni, non-graduating attendees, parents, grandparents, faculty, staff, and athletic season ticket holders, athletic booster club members, etc. just to name a few.
- Demographic Categories: can include, but are not limited to, variables such as gender, year of birth, level of education, marital status, number of children and living or deceased.

- Geographic Segmentation Categories: generally includes variables such as zip or mailing code(s), state, telephone area code, country codes, etc.
- Student Activities Categories: can include, but are not limited to, Varsity Athletics participation, Intramural Athletics participation, student government or student activity clubs, and sororities or fraternities, amongst others.

Overall, these *soft data* elements should be converted into numeric data. Moreover, "if it is possible to extract the data in that format, it will save you considerable time" (Birkholtz 2008, p.152). For example, in the demographic category of *living or deceased*, you can use 1/0 fields where 1 = living and 0 = deceased (Wylie 2004). Perhaps in the demographic category of *year of birth*, you can use 1/0 fields where 1 = people born between 1920 and 1979 and 0 = people born between 1980 and the present. Taken a step further, a significant amount of money can be efficiently saved by incorporating this type of predictive modeling system (Wylie 2004).

If the budget only allows $7,000 for physical postal mailings and it has been five years since the demographic *living/deceased category* has been updated, it is possible to save a significant amount of money by utilizing technology to *omit* the deceased individuals from the database. Furthermore, utilizing technology in this area will allow you to *screen out* wasteful spending and ultimately narrow and identify who among your constituency are most likely to donate, and therefore target your resources more effectively and efficiently. Technology has the ability to enhance the diverse communication mediums of the athletic development office. Traditional methods that are costly are telephone communication, postal mailings, which can be expensive, as well as travel expenses, which all should be used judiciously.

However, incorporating a sophisticated e-mail client or perhaps a social networking medium such as Facebook, Twitter or some other Internet networking communication method can be a cost-effective way of communicating your mission and goals. Therefore, the objective of this process is two-fold. First, identify the constituency and rate them on elements with regards to their linkage to your sport organization, their ability to make gifts, and the degree of interest they have in your sport organization. For example, as was mentioned previously, this can be accomplished through the utilization of a five-point scale. Second, pick out the people who are the *most likely* to give gifts of money *frequently*. This can be accomplished by identifying relevant *hard data* and *soft data* elements. By assigning numbers to these predictors of giving, the use of statistics can enable you to do the following:

- To find out which of the hundreds and hundreds of names in your database to present for further screening, if you are attempting to select the donors who are most likely to be cultivated for a major gift.
- To figure out very efficiently who among your alumni that were born between 1920 and 1979 are most promising candidates to make a major donation and as such, effectively target your resources.
- To identify which of those major donors your athletic director or other influential stakeholders of the athletic program should be focusing on.

In the end, this statistical process is a *tool* that can aid you and your athletic department to make good, accurate and efficient decisions about your donors and prospective donors.

Evaluating the Results

Periodic evaluation is needed to ensure success over the long term because the activity of *evaluating* is a worthwhile learning tool as well as a planning tool. For example, it is quite logical to assess the elements of the fundraiser that worked well, and formulate a simple and comprehensive tally sheet to indicate those activities that need to be reinforced and/or continued, as well as those practices that were mediocre and/or did not work at all. Moreover, there are fundamental ways in which to measure the finite or *hard data* elements that can include, but are not limited to, the following:

- total amount of money contributed to the sports program
- total number of contributors
- total number of booster club members
- the number of mailings (postal and electronic)
- the total number of phone solicitations
- the total number of ticket sales for special events

- the total number of corporate sponsorships (financial and in-kind)
- the total number of applications submitted to granting institutions.

Generally, the most relevant and unmistakable measurement of the success of a fundraising initiative is figuring out whether you have raised the funds that were originally predetermined at the outset. While this is a fairly simple calculation, evaluating success in sports fundraising involves much more than the ending dollar figures. In addition to evaluating the results of the fundraising activities and determining whether or not they should be continued, improved upon or terminated, assessments also need to be made regarding the *individual efforts* and the *procedures* that would have influenced the results.

How well did the Director of Athletics work with the fundraising committee, booster club membership or the volunteers? Were the fundraising goals that were agreed upon achievable? Were those goals reached? Were the goals modified midstream? Was the schedule adhered to? Was there conflict among any groups or individuals? Were there too many people involved or too few? Was there anything new about this fundraiser that could be repeated or done again? These are just a small sample of the many questions to consider when evaluating the individual efforts and procedures within the sports fundraiser. The key point to remember here is to attempt to pinpoint the origin of success or failure within the fundraising project and to learn from it. This aspect can be very enlightening and what is learned at this stage should facilitate future planning strategies. If the evaluation methodology is too complex of an undertaking for your sport organization, perhaps an alternative would be "to engage the services of a consultant to conduct a development audit" (Weinstein 1999, p.284).

In general, bringing in a neutral third-party consultant allows for an unbiased evaluation of the sport organization's development/fundraising program. This effort of hiring a consultant can be beneficial in the long term as it will provide the sport organization with an accurate portrayal of the hard data elements combined with the individual procedures. Without proper assessment either in-house or by a third party, future fundraising frustration and potential failure is imminent. Finally, keep in mind that evaluation of sports fundraising should be viewed as "an ongoing activity, program or process" (Stier 2001, p.18). All too often, especially among youth and interscholastic programs, evaluation is viewed as a daunting, tedious and impractical task.

THE FUNDRAISING CYCLE

There are multiple variations of this process, the majority of which are cyclical in their construct and philosophy. In an interview, Bob Arkeilpane, former University of Cincinnati Deputy Director of Athletics, spoke of various fundraising techniques and philosophies, including those previously illustrated by Henry "Hank" Rosso. One of the key concepts to keep in mind here is that there can be a point in the cycle where failure can occur if the gift is asked for too soon in the process.

The following list is a simplified version of the fundraising cycle that Arkeilpane shared in our conversation, consisting of five components:

- develop the constituency
- cultivate the donor
- make the "ask" and get the gift
- steward the donor
- renew the gift and repeat the process.

Develop the Constituency

In essence, the concept to remember about constituency development is that the sport organization should seek to be in harmony with the needs and interests of those individuals who have a bond with the organization. In other words, the key is to have those interested persons brought closer to the mission of the sport organization. Certainly the LAI Principle must be present with this group. The best donors can be identified by their past giving behavior as well as by demonstrating the components of the LAI Principle. At this point in constituency development, you will want to bring on as many influential people as you can who have a *connection* and bring them together with your Board of Trustees as well as your volunteer base. This is a *critical point* of the development process that leads to cultivation. If these vital aspects are missed or ignored, or not carefully orchestrated, and the gift is asked for too early on in the process, failure can occur. The primary functions of bringing the volunteer base together are the following: first, they are going to help you plan. Once they feel that their input is has been heard and deemed important, they will ultimately feel even more connected to the fundraising project and will develop a sense of ownership. Second, you will have the opportunity to take what the volunteers have told you and weave this information carefully into the plan. The next objective is to find people who are *centers of influence* that can aid in cultivating the prospect.

Cultivate the Donor

Especially at the intercollegiate athletic level, donor cultivation is an ongoing process that primarily concerns the athletic program development personnel working together to establish a positive relationship with each donor. The preexisting knowledge should be that the more robust the relationship, the larger and potentially more frequent the gift will be. In addition to implementing an LAI rating system, as discussed previously, if the system generates a strong enough LAI score, then it is imperative for athletic development officers to seek the best possible solicitor–prospect designations. This is when people who are *centers of influence* can take advantage of solicitors' peer contacts, relationships/network, and leverage. Prospects are more likely to give when solicitation comes from the *right person*. Ultimately this should be someone they respect and who can make a credible and personal case for supporting the athletic program. Volunteers' involvement with the cultivating phase "can provide assistance in opening doors, endorsing proposals, making corporate or personal gifts, signing thank-you letters, and participating in other recognition activities" (Burlingame 2003, p.183).

In sum, if a prospect is being cultivated for a major gift of $2,000,000 and the *ask* is from someone who is not a *center of influence* with that person, it will be much more likely for that prospect to say no, compared to if it were from someone they respect and are personally familiar with.

Ideally, an *existing donor* should be carefully considered and coached as the *right person* to make *the ask* if they are a center of influence for the prospect being cultivated for the $2 million dollar gift solicitation.

This decision is ultimately orchestrated by the athletic department's fundraising executive, who serves to plan and manage the entire fundraising process. Researching and finding the person who is to be designated as the *center of influence* can take months or perhaps even years, depending on the magnitude of the gift being sought by the athletic organization. Again, ideally the person designated as the *center of influence* will continue to cultivate the prospect because he or she is passionately devoted to the athletic program both emotionally and financially and because of this, it makes it more difficult for the prospect to say no.

As was mentioned previously, a significant function within this phase of the cycle is to take what the volunteers have told you and *that information* should be carefully woven into the plan. Also, finding people who are *centers of influence* that can aid in cultivating the prospect is important. The cultivation phase is also when conceptualizing the creation and *feasibility* of the "table of gifts" takes place. If the fundraising goal for the athletic department is to raise ten million dollars, gifts of this nature always come in the form of a pyramid or *table*. A "table of gifts" needs to be prearranged by the stakeholders and athletic development staff. For the purposes of basic illustration, the $2 million mentioned earlier would be the top of the table. Then, two gifts of $1.5million, three gifts of $1 million and then four gifts of $500,000, all totaling $10 million dollars, would follow (see Figure 4.2).

The athletic fundraising campaign gift table and the associated number of gifts needs to be carefully planned by all stakeholders/volunteers, and can vary from one sport organization to another. However, regardless of the number and size of each gift being considered, the appropriate *ratio of prospects* needed for one gift should be *at least* 4:1. Therefore, if you have a table of gifts with two gifts of $1.5 million, you need to have eight names of people who have the linkage, ability, and interest because chances are, it's going to take four *asks* to get one gift among these prospects. Furthermore, if the sport organization has a table of gifts and is unable to produce at least a 4:1 ratio of active, cultivated names of prospects for each gift, you can determine very quickly the success or failure of the fundraising campaign.

Number of gifts	$ amount	Minimum number of cultivated prospects	Cumulative $ total
1	2 million	4	2 million
2	1.5 million	8	3 million
3	1 million	12	3 million
4	½ million	16	2 million

Figure 4.2 The Athletic Fundraising Campaign Table of Gifts Example

Make the Ask and Get the Gift

This fourth part of the cycle, also referred to as the *solicitation*, is when the idiom of "where the rubber meets the road" becomes very relevant to sports fundraising. Overall, Seiler states "The solicitation step calls for already committed donors to visit personally those from whom gifts will be sought. The current donor makes the case for the organization, explains his or her own level of commitment, and invites the prospective donor to join in the fulfillment of the mission by making a charitable gift" (2003, p.29). Taken as a whole, personal/face-to-face solicitation is considered as the most effective strategy in raising major gifts. Once the prospect's *center of influence* or peer has properly asked to get the gift at the right time, under the right circumstances and the prospect has agreed, the next phase of the cycle is to *steward the donor.*

Steward the Donor

There are a variety of definitions to describe the concept of *stewardship* relative to fundraising. According to Conway, it means "being responsible for something valuable on behalf of someone who has entrusted it to our care" (2003, p.432). Stewardship involves *ethical accountability*; good stewardship in fundraising goes beyond the general responsibility of donor recognition/acknowledgement of gifts. It also incorporates a *relationship-building strategy* that encourages future giving. Stewarding the donor, especially one that is donating a significantly large gift, should not be viewed as a *business transaction*, but rather as a genuine and appropriate expression of appreciation that is *personalized.*

For example, if the prospect had made a contribution to the athletic program for two million dollars, sending out an e-mail or a form letter thanking them for their gift is an inappropriate method of stewarding the donor. Despite the fact that throughout the early parts of the cycle, the prospect had been statistically categorized thorough the utilization of a prospect rating system as well as judicious planning and cultivation strategies, once the gift has been made, major donors should not be treated as a number. Rather, donors at that kind of level should be getting personal phone calls from high-ranking personnel as well as personalized/hand-written letters of gratitude that are prompt, meaningful and sincere. Donors who contribute at that kind of level should be viewed as valued partners. In fact, instead of placing their name on a wall plaque in the gymnasium, find a special gift, within reason, that has particular meaning to them and is specifically tailored for that donor.

Overall, these donors should also receive updates, such as *insider newsletters* or other forms of exclusive communication that demonstrate how their gift is being used and the positive impact it has made on the sport organization as a whole. By genuinely communicating with your major donors on a personalized basis, you are letting your donors know how their gift is being used as well as connecting with them and respecting them. Finally, in the long term, the better you are at truly stewarding the donor, the closer you will lead them to the core of your sport organization as a valued partner.

Renew the Gift and Repeat the Process

The success of this phase of the cycle is subject to how well stakeholders/constituents have been educated about the mission of the athletic program and conditioned to provide financial support. In terms of gift renewal, Seiler states, "Properly thanking donors, reporting the use of gifts, and demonstrating wise stewardship of contributed funds makes renewal of the gift possible" (2003, p.29). Donors to your athletic organization have already exemplified their commitment by the financial offerings they have made on your behalf. Moreover, stewarding the gift appropriately means treating your donors with genuine respect, sincere appreciation, and clearly demonstrating how the gift was used. If that happens, the likelihood is that they will give again. An essential element to keep in mind is to ask your donors if they can help you engage and cultivate others in the fundraising endeavor. People who have contributed major gifts can help you solicit others to donate to your athletic organization. Furthermore, they usually socialize with people who share similar values, beliefs, and also have similar monetary resources. Ultimately, stewardship leads to renewing the gift to the athletic organization which then leads back to developing the constituency, and the cycle can begin again.

THE 90–10 PRINCIPLE

In non-profit fundraising, the 90–10 Principle is often referred to as the 80–20 Pareto Principle, when 20 percent of all donors contribute 80 percent of the total donated money. In intercollegiate athletic fundraising, the principle remains the same, but the ratio is closer to 90–10. In a meeting on 10 July 2009, Arkeilpane indicated that if you want to raise $100,000, then the theory of "let's go get 100 people to give $1,000" absolutely has never ever once worked and it will never work. "Ninety percent of the money in any fundraising campaign comes from ten percent of the people" (Arkeilpane, B. 2009, pers. comm., 10 July).

Therefore, the essential objective to remember is that you need to focus on those people who comprise the ten percent. Taking everything into account, they are the ones that matter the most. Conversely, this is not to suggest that you ignore the other ninety percent, but rather, that larger group of people can be efficiently cultivated through direct mail/e-mail as well as large events. Hence, the ten percent requires *more personal attention and communication* and as part of a cultivation strategy, you need to take the time to understand their background, connection, desires, and their vision, and have them associate with a current donor who is a *center of influence*. These fundraising strategies, when appropriately applied, work well at the collegiate level.

In conclusion, for those involved in youth and high school programs, there are certainly lessons to be learned about this type of fundraising. The approaches presented are a bit more advanced than the typical or traditional methods used to fundraise at the youth/high school levels. Consequently, at the end of this chapter there are application exercises to provide a fundamental framework on how to incorporate these ideas and approaches in an efficient and effective manner, which are applicable to all levels.

FURTHER READING

Azzaro, J. A. (2005) "Understanding a high-performance university development organization: Leadership and best practices", The Ohio State University, available at http://search.proquest.com/docview/3045425957?accountid=2909 (accessed 01/31/12).

Birkholz, Joshua M. (2008) *Fundraising Analytics*, Hoboken, NJ: John Wiley & Sons, Inc.

Dickerson, F. C. (2009) "Writing the voice of philanthropy: How to raise money with words", Claremont University, available at http://search.proquest.com/docview/304864795?accountid=2909 (accessed 01/31/12).

Duronio, M. A. and Loessin, B. A. (1991) *Effective fund raising in higher education: Ten success stories.* San Francisco, CA: Jossey-Bass.

Greenfield, J. M. (1994) *Fundraising fundamentals: A guide to annual giving for professionals and volunteers.* New York: John Wiley & Sons, Inc.

McGuire, J. P. (2003) "Integrating fundraising with academic planning and budgeting: Toward an understanding of strategic fundraising", University of Pennsylvania, available at http://search.proquest.com/docview/305306614?accountid=2909 (accessed 01/31/12).

Meer, J. and Rosen, H. S., (2008) "The impact of athletic performance on alumni giving: An analysis of microdata", *Economics of Education Review*, 28 (3) 287–294.

Miller, M.T. (1993) "Fund Raising for Athletic Programs: Considerations for Success", University of Nebraska available at http://www.eric.ed.gov/PDFS/ED358793.pdf (accessed 01/31/12).

Rosso, Henry A. (2003) *Achieving Excellence in Fundraising* (2nd edn), San Francisco, CA: Jossey-Bass.

Shapiro, S. L. (2008) "Donor loyalty in college athletics: An analysis of relationship fundraising and service quality effects on donor retention", University of Northern Colorado, available at http://search.proquest.com/docview/304541022?accountid=2909 (accessed 01/31/12).

Schmidt, J. C. (2001) "Mining philanthropic data: Models for predicting alumni/us giving at a medium-sized public master's university", University of Minnesota, available at http://search.proquest.com/docview/304705037?accountid=2909 (accessed 01/31/12).

Stinson, J. L. and Howard, D. R. (2004) "Scoreboards vs. mortarboards: Major donor behavior and intercollegiate athletics", *Sport Marketing Quarterly*, 3 (3) 129–140.

——(2007) "Athletic success and private giving to athletic and academic programs at NCAA institutions", *Journal of Sport Management*, 21, 235–264.

Wylie, P. B. (2004) *Data Mining for Fundraisers*, Washington, DC: Council for Advancement and Support of Education.

—— (2008) *Baseball, fundraising, and the 80/20 rule: Studies in data mining*, Washington, DC: Council for Advancement and Support of Education.

APPLICATION/SKILL BUILDING EXERCISE

Exercise applicable for both students and practitioners:

Select a youth sport organization, a high school *or* a college/university athletic department of your choice to examine/study. Based on the geographic location of that institution, make an honest attempt to complete the following four tasks. By completing these tasks in earnest, you will get a sense of the process and skill it takes to identify, rate and convert hard and soft data elements into numeric data.

Create a list of possible internal and external groups of people who could be considered as the *constituency* or *stakeholders* of the athletic/sports program.

Once you have identified your constituency, now try and A) organize them into their specific categories and B) create a rating system utilizing three criteria known as the *Rosso LAI Principle.*

Now that you have identified and rated constituencies based on the LAI Principle, A) identify and list specific *hard data* that would be useful, in addition to *soft data* variables, that could be related to giving among your constituency and B) convert those elements into *numeric data.*

Based on the chapter lesson and the completion of the previous three tasks, how would you go about deciding which people are the most likely to give gifts of money most frequently?

CHAPTER 5

INTERCOLLEGIATE RELATIONSHIP CULTIVATION AND STEWARDSHIP IN FUNDRAISING

The purpose of this chapter is to identify and explain the general philosophy, principles, significant topics and contemporary issues relative to relationship cultivation and stewardship among the intercollegiate athletic fundraising discipline. Another aim of this chapter is to identify and explain the primary types of fundraising campaigns as well as the key components to creating successful feasibility studies in intercollegiate athletics.

In regard to the fundraising activities performed at the intercollegiate athletic level, the identifying term and/or name of this discipline can be described or referred to as *athletic development*, *athletic advancement*, or in some cases the *athletic fund*. Overall, the work that is accomplished can be defined as the identification, proactive management and promotion of an athletic department to its stakeholders. This can involve, but is not limited to, activities associated with relationship cultivation, stewardship and various modes of communication that lead to the acquisition of financial resources. The prevailing theme of this book has been identifying and analyzing the common themes as well as the distinct differences among the fundraising philosophies and the related activities conducted at the intercollegiate level compared to the youth and interscholastic levels. As was mentioned in Chapter 1, compared to youth and interscholastic programs intercollegiate athletic departments in the United States are, for the most part, associated more with dual elements of *return on investment strategies* such as contracted business arrangements with specific marketing and profit-making objectives as well as elements of *philanthropy*. Nevertheless, when it comes to relationship cultivation and stewardship among corporate sponsors or wealthy individual benefactors those that hold the position of *Director of Athletic*

Development or *Sports Marketing Director* should be aware that there are requisite skill sets for the contemporary athletic fundraiser not only to comprehend, but in which to be proficient.

In many cases across the United States, the larger the athletic program, the more specialized the organizational structure becomes in terms of its *departmentalization*. Accordingly, there is no one way in which intercollegiate athletic departments are organized. For example, one intercollegiate athletic program may have the Athletic Development or Athletic Advancement department separate from the Sports Marketing and Promotions department. Moreover, there may be an Assistant Athletic Director for Marketing and Promotions in addition to an Assistant Athletic Director for Development. Conversely, another college sports program may have an Assistant Athletic Director of Sports Finance which oversees all financial activities including marketing and promotions as well as development and/or advancement activities.

Regardless of the organizational orientation, the essential viewpoint to remember here is that there is an interesting, potent, and *symbiotic relationship* between the Athletic Marketing and Promotions department and the Athletic Development and Advancement department. Primarily, the aims of these departments are to maximize involvement and secure funding. Philosophically, both departments are on the *same team* and therefore, are both delegated with the job of identifying, promoting, acquiring and retaining consistent supporters of the athletic program. Furthermore, while they may be separate departments, they generally report to the same administrator who is above them in the organizational hierarchy. Figure 5.1 illustrates this concept visually, which is a basic and fundamental chart that shows them as separate departments, yet which report to the Associate Athletic Director for External Affairs.

ORGANIZATIONAL CHARACTERISTICS OF INTERCOLLEGIATE BOOSTER CLUBS

Historically, the ethical issues related to overzealous boosters at the intercollegiate level and the violation of NCAA rules and regulations led to the NCAA ordering athletic directors to apply a more rigorous implementation of *institutional control* in the early 1990s. This reform

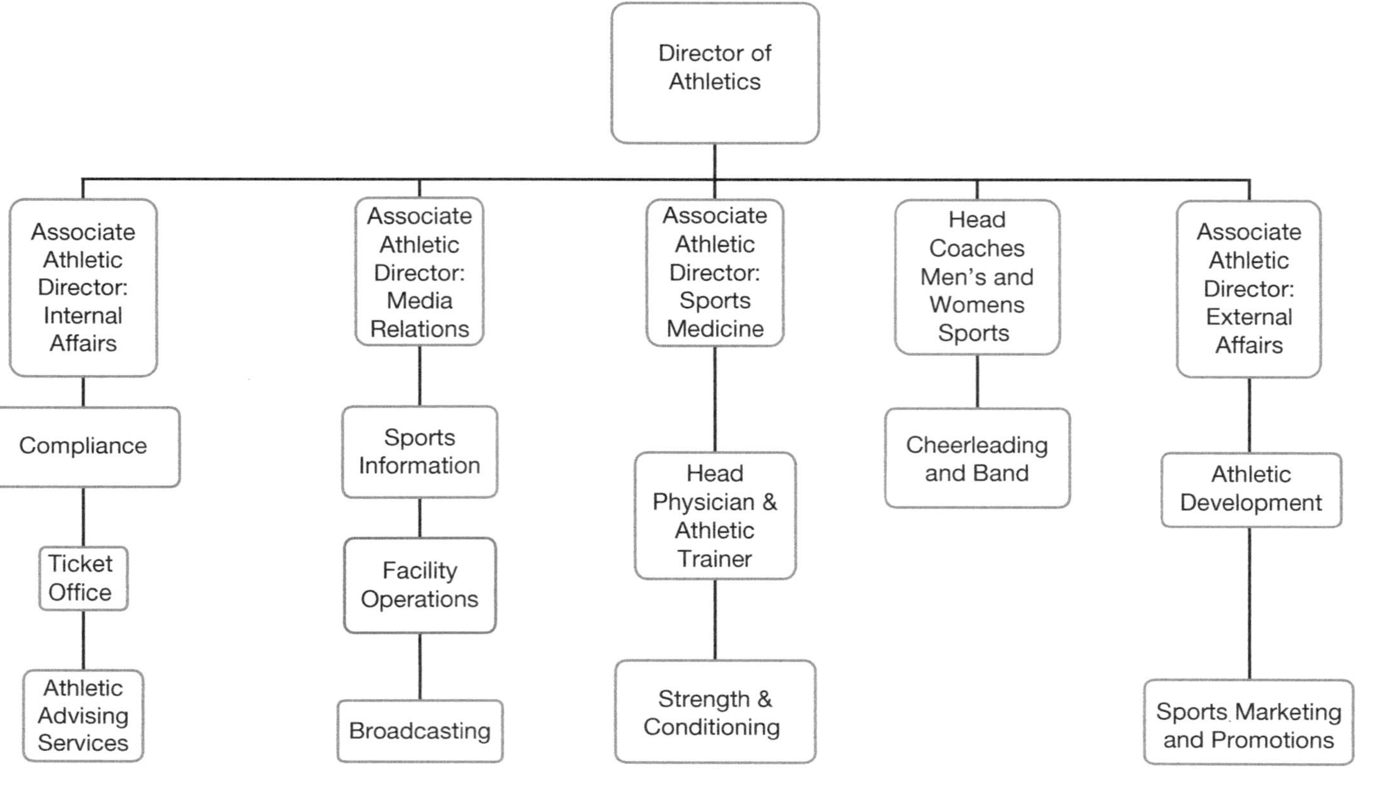

Figure 5.1 Fundamental Intercollegiate Athletic Department Organizational Chart

initiative was made in response to the significant amount of institutions that were not controlling and/or disciplining their athletic boosters from making unlawful monetary gifts to their current or potential student athletes.

According to Howard and Crompton, "In a document titled *Principles of Institutional Control*, first issued in the spring of 1992, athletic programs were mandated to develop and maintain rules-education programs for all constituent groups, including boosters" (2004, p.577). As a result of this mandate, the NCAA provided institutions with detailed and documented guidelines in order to help ensure implementation and compliance. This was despite the fact that *institutional control* of athletic booster groups, especially at the major Division I-A level, is somewhat of an elusive concept.

Consequently, many intercollegiate athletic departments across the nation started the process of either complying with the mandates, or changing their approach to the organization and procedures of their booster clubs. Many successful intercollegiate booster organizations operate as a separate, tax-exempt 501(c) (3) that is independent from the university it represents. Simultaneously, many other universities across the nation, based on the mandates imposed by the NCAA, decided to create their own *in-house* booster clubs. "Under this arrangement, the club 'resides' within the department and is staffed by departmental personnel. This internal booster club model has worked well for many institutions, including Ohio State's Buckeye Club, Iowa's I-Club and Oregon's Duck Athletic Fund" (Howard and Crompton 2004, p.579). Optimistically, the Director of Athletics must act in providing proactive oversight, supervision and institutional control of booster clubs regardless of whether they are separate from the university or *operate in-house.*

THE RETURN ON INVESTMENT ORIENTATION

Relating to intercollegiate athletics, return on investment, also referred to as ROI, is the monetary benefits received from having invested money on a sports sponsorship. An important aspect of fundraising to understand is that in the context of an intercollegiate athletic program, fundraising is a *different activity* compared to corporate sponsorships, as well as a *related activity.* As was pointed out earlier in this chapter, this is where there is a *symbiotic relationship.*

For example, the intent of *corporate sponsorships*, which are usually managed by the Sports Marketing and Promotions department, is for there to be a mutual agreement between the athletic program and the sponsoring business, in which "the company expects tangible commercial benefits in the form of increased visibility and sales and an enhanced image in the marketplace" (Howard and Crompton 2004, p.573). Simultaneously, the intent of athletic fundraising, which is usually managed by the Athletic Development and/or Advancement department, is for there to be a mutual agreement between the athletic program and an *individual donor*. However, the donor would not expect a commercial benefit, having mainly donated for more philanthropic reasons. In essence, "Donors are likely to contribute because of their emotional attachment to a sports organization, whereas corporations are likely to enter a sponsorship based on return on investment considerations" (Howard and Crompton 2004, p.574). While some motivations to donate large amounts of money to an intercollegiate athletic program are, for the most part, benevolent in concept, "the most effective fundraising programs recognize that both psychic rewards such as ego enhancement, and tangible rewards, such as preferred seating privileges, are integral components of donor solicitation" (Howard and Crompton 2004, p.574). Generally, this is where the concept of *quid pro quo* comes into play, which is a form of ROI in athletic fundraising.

Introduced in Chapter 1, if a donor is receiving a benefit in return (i.e. premium tickets, preferred parking space) then, based on Internal Revenue Service rules, only eighty percent of their contribution is tax-deductible. If the donor is truly philanthropic in their gift to the athletic program and they decline to accept the benefits, then they can deduct 100 percent of their contribution. This is certainly a simplified description of the tax implications and the rules of the Internal Revenue Service (IRS).

It is beyond the scope of this text to go into great detail of the tax laws, which are complicated and ever-changing. In the end, it is the responsibility of the Athletic Development department to *inform donors*, usually in writing, that if they accept a benefit, such as preferred seating, then only eighty percent of their gift is tax-deductible, and that they should consult their tax advisors if they require any more information relative to tax laws.

THE THREE TYPES: ANNUAL, MAJOR AND PRINCIPAL

The Annual Campaign

This is also referred to as the *annual fund* in fundraising circles. The primary aim of this type of fundraising campaign is to maximize participation, regardless of the giving level and to accomplish it without spending too much money on postage and telephone costs. Furthermore, "your focus is mostly on mail and phone campaigns; your prospects include both donors and non-donors; and the specific 'ask' is not a huge amount of money" (Wylie 2004, p.3). Moreover, it costs more money to acquire a new donor than it does to maintain or renew someone who has given in the past. This type of campaign can be considered as a *high volume–low dollar activity*. Giving patterns to be expected at this level are approximately twenty-five percent. Therefore, as a fundamental example, in asking 100 alumni who are perhaps former student athletes, the likelihood is that twenty-five of them will say yes and make a gift. In an annual campaign, a really good first-time gift is about fifty dollars from a non-donor.

In intercollegiate athletics, creativity and the aggressive pursuit of maximizing participation for the annual campaign can take on a variety of forms with unique strategies. For example, in an effort to broaden its membership base and encourage new donor participation, the University of Cincinnati's UCATS Department, which is the primary fundraising arm of the entire athletic department, implemented a strategy that *rewards* current members by referring new supporters, which is called the "UCATS Each One Reach One New Member Referral Program" (UCATS New Member Referral Program n.d.).

The program provides members of UCATS opportunities to add more value to their membership by incorporating a *priority points system*. In a nutshell, the *rewards* are such that the more new members that are referred to UCATS for membership, the more additional priority points are given to current members towards the goal of moving up the scale of the UCATS Priority Points System. This approach is a *ranking system* and "provides an equitable and systematic method of providing benefits to donors for their financial investments in UC Athletics. Priority Points determine selection order for season ticket seat assignments, away-game allocation, parking, seat improvements, and other special events or activities" (UCATS Priority Points System n.d., p.1). This program and system of maximizing participation for this specific athletic annual fund is unique and successful. Wisely, the University of Cincinnati's athletic department applied creativity by empowering and rewarding current members with the framework to recruit and refer prospects, and in such a way, keeps the annual giving expenses low.

The Major Campaign

This aspect of fundraising is somewhat of an elusive process. What constitutes a major gift made to one intercollegiate athletic institution can be quite different in comparison to another intercollegiate athletic institution. As a result, there aren't any well-defined criteria for what represents a major gift. This type of campaign can be considered as a *low volume–high dollar activity*. Furthermore, a major gift needs to fit the circumstances in which the athletic department exists from a historical perspective of how well they have performed in raising funds. It is very unreasonable to set the major gift category at $1 million if the athletic development department is struggling to find donors who can contribute $500.

Therefore, when attempting to define and/or set the *entry level* for a major gift, a good strategy is to figure out what the highest amount annual gift that your intercollegiate athletic department has received. For example, let's assume that a small-sized intercollegiate athletic program typically receives $2,500 as their largest annual gift. In order to set a *major gift range*, one should multiply the largest gift by five to ten times larger than what is generally received. In this instance, this small-sized intercollegiate athletic program should set their major gift range between $12,500 and $25,000. Similarly, if the highest typical gift for a larger institution is $100,000, then their range for a major gift should be set somewhere around $500,000 to $1,000,000. As it was pointed out in Chapter 4, regardless of the number and size of each gift being considered, the appropriate *ratio of prospects* needed for one gift should be at least 4:1. Referring back to the original example, if the small-sized athletic program has determined that they will have one major gift of $25,000, there should be, at the very least, four names of cultivated donors who have the *linkage, ability* and *interest* in the mission and work of the athletic department. Once the size of major gifts has been determined, another aspect to understand and appreciate is what motivates donors to make major gifts.

At this particular juncture, it is important to understand some basic factors that can help explain *why* a person gives a gift of significant size to an intercollegiate athletic program. There has been a steady and substantial shift in what motivates donor behavior. Ultimately, it hinges on the concept of wanting to be *involved* with the athletic program, more so than wanting their name on the entrance into the weightlifting facility, for example. While recognition and other *customary* stewardship provisions such as exclusive parties and other *wining and dining events* are standard practice in many intercollegiate athletic development programs across the United States, there are a growing number of wealthy individuals who shy away from public displays of recognition and the ancillary activities that go with it. Motivation comes from within the individual and as such, it is the job of the athletic development and/or athletic advancement office to figure out what motivates their cultivated donors. Then, the appropriate environment needs to be *created* so that their motivation to donate will flourish. This requires *listening* to your donor. What do they *value* most? The better you can become at truly listening to your donors as to what they value most may yield favorable results that are unrelated to the aforementioned public displays of recognition.

For example, perhaps the major donor truly values diversity and simultaneously wants to help student athletes succeed just as much in the classroom as they do on the playing field. Perhaps the donor sees *value* in putting their donation toward academic tutoring services. As a result, the physical manifestation of their *gift in action* is what motivates them. This type of *involvement* not only impacts upon the potential of keeping this major donor in the future, but also may motivate them to reach out to their friends and colleagues who share those same values and help in cultivating them to give to the intercollegiate athletic program as well. Finding *true motivation* doesn't come from a website, an article, or a spreadsheet; the only true reliable resource is the donor themselves. Arkeilpane indicated that gifts always come with strings attached. People always have a particular interest. It may be football, it may be basketball ... it may be scholarships. It might be that they are interested in athletics, but they want it to go towards academics and as a result they want the money to go toward the academic advising center (Arkeilpane, B. 2009, pers. comm., 10 July). As a result, it is incumbent upon the athletic department to respect the donor's request to use the money in the way they intend. If it is well-reported and clearly *demonstrated* that the donor's gift went to where they intended it to go, it's going to be much easier to approach the donor for a second gift in future encounters.

A thorough exploration and analysis of *donor motivation*, as well as resources that provide theoretical explanations and key drivers of this and relationship marketing in athletics, will be illustrated in Chapter 8.

The Principal Campaign

In most instances across the United States, *principal gifts* are the types that not only exceed major gifts in terms of monetary size, but also in terms of the impact they make on the entire educational institution. Some educational institutions may define principal gifts as more than five million dollars. While the monetary magnitude of the gift size is significant, "These are rare gifts in the life of an institution in which the institution's values become so exemplified in the benefactor's act of generosity that the gift itself serves to sharpen, refine, and, in a meaningful sense, rededicate the entirety of the institution to its deepest core values" (Schubert 2002, p.105). Also referred to as *ultimate gifts*, they "represent an act of giving over the largest share of one's life work to a given cause or purpose" (Schubert 2002, p.106). Therefore, a clearly defined mission is absolutely *essential* for an athletic department if they desire to receive a gift of a lifetime. For example, in 2003, the University of Cincinnati received a gift of $10.2 million from Richard E. Lindner, a Cincinnati Ohio businessman and philanthropist, who made it financially possible for the university to enhance existing, as well as create, state of the art, world-class athletic training facilities. Bob Goin, who was the University of Cincinnati Director of Athletics at the time of the gift in 2003 stated, "Dr. Lindner's generosity toward the university hit an all-time high in his gift that enables us to have a state of the art athletic center. This facility will provide all the necessary services for our student athletes to compete at a Division

I level. We are proud that Varsity Village and the center will bear his name" (Hathaway 2003, p.1).

As was detailed in Chapter 4, Hank Rosso's *LAI Principle* is a fundamental tenet in fundraising, and it is good fundraising practice to identify and then target prospective donors who display all three criteria. Moreover, when it comes to principal gift cultivation, the *link* is considered the vital goal, and it is by no mistake that it is listed first. "The goal of principal gift cultivation will always be forging a long series of ever-closer links between benefactor and institution over many years, steadily moving toward a convergence point where the values of benefactor and institution can be said to fully merge" (Schubert 2002, p.109). Accordingly, the fundamental objective to keep in mind here is that the *link* between the mission and values of the intercollegiate athletic department must be in accord with the life values of the benefactor when it comes to principal gift cultivation.

CAPITAL CAMPAIGNS AND ENDOWMENTS

This is an aspect of fundraising that requires proper planning and organization and should be executed judiciously. A *capital campaign* is a fundraising endeavor that has the primary aim of raising enough money for either the construction of a new sports facility or perhaps the renovation of an existing sport facility. Capital campaigns are often referred to as "bricks and mortar" activities. Intercollegiate athletic programs in the United States conduct capital campaigns to purchase sports equipment, specific machinery or other ancillary assets. Capital campaigns generate the funds to be spent on the specific construction project all at once, and because of this they are rarely repeated, and are raised and spent in the short term.

Endowments are generally viewed as more of a long-term investment in the support of an athletic program. Moreover, the endowment gift is large enough to generate income through *annual interest*. "The principal or original amount donated is left untouched in a perpetual interest-bearing account providing an ongoing source of revenue for the athletic department" (Howard and Crompton 2004, p.574). Therefore, an *endowment campaign* is a fundraising endeavor that has the primary aim of *investing* as opposed to *spending*, and is generally utilized by intercollegiate athletic departments for full athletic scholarships offered to student athletes to offset the costs of education, in terms of tuition, books, as well as room and board. Overall, the *endowment funds* are utilized for general operation intentions such as athletic scholarships and/or for capital disbursements, such as new sport facility construction and/or renovation. Moreover, "As in any endowment, the interest generated each year on the principal money donated is used toward tuition, etc.' (Stier 2001, p.116).

For example, at the University of Michigan in 2009, "athletic department officials estimate that 130 scholarships across all sports are at least partially funded by private contributions" (Fish 2009, p.1). At Stanford University, the majority of the athletic scholarships and many of the coaching positions are endowed in perpetuity by individual gifts to the athletic program. Often referred to as an *endowment portfolio*, this definitively aids in keeping athletic programs competitive and helps insulate them through tough and turbulent economic times. Moreover, many athletic departments across the United States took the *endowed-chair idea* from the academic fundraising domain. For example, in intercollegiate football, the position of quarterback, wide-receiver or perhaps even the special teams coach, are endowed at most major athletic programs across the United States. "On the college level, this might be termed an Endowed Chair for Coaching, similar to the Endowed Chair for Physics–paying for the salary of a specific coach rather than the physics professor" (Stier 2001, p.116).

As a result, scholarships and coaching positions endowed in perpetuity are happening on many intercollegiate campuses in the United States. During times when the economy is tumultuous, coupled with the rising/inflationary costs of a college education, having endowed scholarships and coaching positions in perpetuity is a boon. All things considered, many other institutions are looking at building their endowment portfolios in order to help keep their athletic programs competitive and viable.

FEASIBILITY STUDIES

These are planned activities that athletic departments utilize in identifying potential donors, organizational leaders (both formal and informal), as well as internal and external environmental factors that will attract support and commitment. Also referred to as a campaign study or perhaps in some cases a *market survey*, the general view is that feasibility studies are a way of testing the economic waters to see if it is safe to swim toward donors. The *timing* of this initiative can potentially vary from six months all the way up to an entire year, depending upon the size and scope of the fundraising project. Overall, this component is a *test*, or an attempt to determine the success of the athletic fundraising initiative prior to actually committing all of the financial and human resources needed for the project. All of the work that was conducted in identifying and cultivating the constituency can now be applied in this trial or test phase.

There are two really important components to consider when undertaking feasibility studies. First, as previously illustrated in Chapter 1, the constituency model helps identify and ultimately aid in drawing key people to the *core* of the model. Therefore, those people who demonstrate a strong bond to the organization/athletic department should now be considered as potential interviewees, survey-takers or to take part in a focus group in the feasibility study.

Secondly, it should provide an accurate portrayal of the economic climate and reveal the number of *other* charitable organizations that are within the same region who could be potentially soliciting the same individuals that are on your list. Non-profit charitable organizations pose a significant challenge to raising funds. There are a significant number of charitable organizations whose mission and purpose are to improve the lives of the people they serve and therefore they provide compelling cases for support. These charitable organizations within the same regional area of your athletic department are out there soliciting the disposable income of the same individuals you have spent time identifying and cultivating. Therefore, one of the aims/intents of the feasibility study is to help determine who and/or what those external competitors happen to be.

One of the key objectives of the feasibility study is to enhance the decision-making process by providing such important data of the aforementioned components. By being aware and knowledgeable about these factors, circumstances, and economic conditions will eventually help the athletic department strategically make better decisions. Taken as a whole, the intention here is to "make better decisions and resolve differences of opinions about what to do, why to do it, how to do it, when to do it, who should do it and how well to do it" (Dunlop 2002, p.95). This aspect of the feasibility study can be conducted in a variety of ways, and can be done in a cost-effective manner, both in terms of financial and human resources. For example, many institutions of higher education in the United States bring in a neutral third-party *consultant* to review the *readiness* of the athletic department to conduct a successful fundraising campaign.

In sum, the consultant will, depending on the size and scope of the project, conduct interviews, administer surveys or organize focus groups among the aforementioned stakeholders of the athletic program. These core groups to be interviewed can include, but are not limited to, the following:

- Athletic Development Staff Members
- Board of Directors and Administration/Management
- Major Donors and Select Volunteers

Consequently, the consultant will then analyze the level of commitment/resources as well as request a list of current major donors to the athletic program, current prospects, potential volunteers as well as other key stakeholders of the athletic program. The chief goal of this process by the consultant is three-fold. First, it should provide the athletic department with an understanding of how the study was conducted in terms of its process. It should detail *who, what, where, when, why* and *how* the interviews/surveys/focus groups were carried out.

Second, it should provide the athletic department with an *accurate* depiction of how the participants felt about the proposed fundraising initiative as well as their *perceptions* of the athletic department as a whole. The main point here is the concept of *accuracy of perception*. The use of consultants brings objectivity to the process and "allows potential donors to speak candidly about their interest in the project and their potential financial participation" (Weinstein 1999, p.33). Therefore, a neutral third-party consultant will hopefully bring sound judgment to the analysis compared to analyses that are done *in-house* by employees. The reason for this is that there are potential pitfalls of staff members who may anticipate an *exaggerated degree* of financial participation compared to what the donor actually states or commits to supporting. Thus, the athletic department should use the *feedback* provided from the feasibility study and determine whether enough donors exist to make the campaign successful.

Finally, whether or not they have the infrastructure in place to support committing their full financial and human resources towards the campaign should also be revealed through the study. To make the feasibility process more cost-effective for the institution, some athletic departments implement a more financially pragmatic approach to feasibility studies. Smaller-sized intercollegiate athletic departments generally do not have the financial resources to hire a neutral third-party consultant. Therefore, these athletic departments have to be resourceful and reach out for free help among specific departments on campus.

For example, Stier states, "College or university athletic departments have only to go across campus and request assistance from the department of business or marketing within the same institution" (2001, p.146). The benefits of this type of *partnering* allows the athletic department to keep their costs down while simultaneously providing a significant hands-on learning experience for students who are studying this aspect as part of their college education. This kind of collaborative research project can prove beneficial because many professors on college campuses have significant experience with survey research and skilled statistical analyses. Furthermore, the students provide valuable labor through the input of data as well as other tasks such as survey administration and other pieces of *market segmentation* that the intercollegiate athletic department regards as important.

In conclusion, whether a school's athletic department decides to hire a neutral third-party consultant or reach out and utilize the resourcefulness of those students on campus, the fundamental point is that the feasibility study is a *purposeful instrument* that produces a meaningful decision-making assessment for administrators. It enables them to determine whether to move forward with a fundraising project or whether to table the decision for a while until the time and conditions are right to reconsider. In the end, the feasibility study is a great tool that can and will have a significant impact on fundraising projects now and in the future.

FURTHER READING

Burlingame, D. (1997) *Critical issues in fundraising*, New York, NY: John Wiley & Sons, Inc.

Coughlin, C. C. and Erekson, O.H. (1985) "Contributions to intercollegiate athletic programs: Further evidence", *Social Science Quarterly*, 66, 194–202.

DiConsiglio, J. (2010) "The way we ask now", *Currents*, 36 (3) 42–46, 48.

Duderstadt, J. (2000) *Intercollegiate athletics and the American university*, Ann Arbor, MI: University of Michigan Press.

Hicks, P. W. (2006) "An exploration of capital campaign team organization, functioning, and fundraising success", University of Michigan, available at http://search.proquest.com/docview/305304898?accountid=2909 (accessed 01/31/12).

Kelly, K. S. (1998) *Effective Fundraising Management*, Mahwah, NJ: Lawrence Erlbaum Associates, Inc.

Mahony, D., Gladden, J. and Funk, D. (2003) "Examining Athletic Donors at NCAA Division I Institutions", *International Journal of Sport Management*, 7 (1) 9–28.

Newman, R. H. (2000) "Eleven must dos for a successful capital or endowment fund campaign", *Fundraising Management*, available at http://www.allbusiness.com/specialty-businesses/non-profit-businesses/487645-1.html (accessed 01/31/12).

Penry, J. C. (2008) "Forecasting the financial trends facing intercollegiate athletic programs of public institutions as identified by athletic directors of the ACC, Big 12 and SEC conferences", Texas A & M University, available at http://search.proquest.com/docview/304331120?accountid=2909 (accessed 01/31/12).

Plinske, P. (2000) "Raising Friends, Raising Funds", *Athletic Management*, Oct–Nov, 33–39.

Reckseen, D. M. and Poole, T. R. (1996) "The anatomy of an endowment/capital campaign", *Fundraising Management*, 27 (6) 14.

Veazey, K. (2011) "Ole miss to unveil $150 million fundraising drive for athletic facilities", United States, Washington: McClatchy-Tribune Information Services, available at http://search.proquest.com/docview/881651952?accountid=2909 (accessed 01/31/12).

Weinstein, S. (1999) *The Complete Guide to Fundraising Management*, New York, NY: John Wiley & Sons Inc.

Witkin, B. and Altschuld, J. (1995) *Planning and Conducting Needs Assessment: A Practical Guide*, Thousand Oaks, CA: Sage Publications.

Wolverton, B. (2009) "For athletics, a billion-dollar goal line", *The Chronicle of Higher Education*, 55 (20), A.1–n/a available at http://search.proquest.com/docview/214638616?accountid=2909 (accessed 01/31/12).

APPLICATION/SKILL BUILDING EXERCISE

Exercise 1: for students

Select a college/university of your choice to examine/study. Make an effort to contact the Director of Athletic Development or Athletic Advancement at that particular college/university. Set up a face-to-face interview or perhaps a telephone interview based on the availability/schedule of the Director of Athletic Development. Based on the chapter lesson regarding *relationship cultivation and stewardship*; engage the Director of Athletic Development to answer the following four questions listed below. Additionally, *create* four distinctive questions of your own based on *your comprehension and interest* in the subject. Document their responses relative to their experience and knowledge about:

- The Athletic Development Director's perception of what criteria define/constitute an annual gift, a major gift, and a principal or ultimate gift at their institution.
- The Athletic Development Director's perception of the skill sets necessary to effectively cultivate and manage annual gifts, major gifts and/or principal gifts.
- The Athletic Development Director's perception as to creative programs aimed at broadening their membership base and encouraging new donor participation.
- The Athletic Development Director's perception of feasibility studies and what pieces of data or other market segmentation elements are important to them.

Exercise 2: for practitioners

Based on the chapter lesson regarding *relationship cultivation and stewardship*, attempt to answer the following areas of inquiry as genuinely and candidly as possible:

- What criteria define/constitute an annual gift, a major gift, and a principal or ultimate gift at your institution?
- What type(s) of training do you provide for employees? What training approaches have you experienced that effectively cultivates and manages annual gifts, major gifts and/or principal gifts?
- Identify and describe any creative programs aimed at broadening your membership base and encouraging new donor participation (i.e. priority points systems, affinity or loyalty-type programs aimed at creating platforms that can be monetized and developed).
- When planning for a fundraising drive, what pieces of data or other market segmentation elements are vital to your organization before you commit resources to it? Does your institution utilize third-party consultants? How likely would it be to partner with a department on campus (such as the Sport Management Department) to conduct a collaborative research project?

CHAPTER 6

YOUTH AND INTERSCHOLASTIC RELATIONSHIP CULTIVATION AND STEWARDSHIP

The intent of this chapter is to identify and explain the essential aspects of athletic fundraising and relationship cultivation as well as stewardship among the youth and interscholastic athletic fundraising discipline. The primary areas and contemporary issues faced by interscholastic athletic programs that will be addressed are booster groups and the concept of *quid pro quo*; symbiotic relationships between youth sport and interscholastic programs, sponsorships/third-party marketing agencies; and the importance of alumni outreach strategies.

As previously detailed in Chapter 2, there are a diverse number of reasons why booster clubs or *external support groups* are needed, and various different ways that they are organized and managed. In the United States, while there are many well-organized clubs at the interscholastic level that financially support the athletic teams and the associated activities in their respective communities from an *organizational perspective*, there are many other booster clubs across America that can be characterized as a *house of cards* due to the inevitable change, transition and/or turnover in their organizational make-up of volunteers/parents. While the booster club hierarchy or organizational structure has remained fairly consistent in terms of title and description, as sport programs have evolved over the last fifty years, the fundraising activities have experienced an increase in scope.

BOOSTERS AND CONTEMPORARY FUNDRAISING DYNAMICS

Concurrent to the amount of transition and turnover among high school booster clubs, and based on many years of research and experience in the interscholastic athletics domain, there appears to be five distinct yet connected contemporary dynamics that have impacted the work of booster clubs when it comes to raising significant amounts of revenue.

These five significant dynamics, discounting other possibilities, are the following:

- managing public perception
- the importance of good public relations
- the importance of 501(c) (3) Federal Tax Exempt Status and linkage to financial institutions
- cultivating areas of specialty among your fundraising committee
- identifying and managing quid pro quo strategies.

When it comes to discussions about finances and *budgets* within public school-based interscholastic athletics, conversations will generally gravitate towards whether or not taxpayer money is involved. In a significant number of school districts across America, many athletic directors have either already adopted or are considering adopting *pay to participate* policies in response to budget cuts by their individual school districts. As a result, pressure has trickled down to the athletic directors who work closely with booster clubs to raise enough money not only to update worn-out uniforms, but in many cases, ensure program survival. The effect of cutting sports/athletic programs has a significant impact on various segments of the community and other industries as well. Without specific sport programs at the interscholastic level, the negative fallout of not supporting athletics has been well-documented. For example, Up2Us, a New York-based advocacy group that serves as a unifying voice for youth sports organizations, estimates that the nation's high schools cut at least $2 billion in funding for athletics in 2008–9. While that figure is based on a small and select sample, the researcher who signed off on it, assistant professor Brian Greenwood at Cal Poly, San Luis Obispo, says he now believes it has grown to "10 times more than that" (King 2010, pp.15–16).

Moreover, this situation has led to an increase of *societal costs*, and the group argues that the cutting of sports leads to "higher dropout rates, more teen pregnancies, and increased teen violence" (King 2010, p.18). This economic meltdown at the interscholastic level has also impacted local merchants, restaurateurs as well as sporting good suppliers who all benefit from healthy youth sport/interscholastic athletic programs. Cutting sports programs can *worsen* the effect on the local economy, as athletic participants, parents and spectators who would normally buy merchandise, food, or some type of sports equipment would dramatically decrease. Overall, it is a situation that has backed many school district administrations into a corner. Therefore, "with tax rolls shrinking and school budgets bleeding, many of the nation's harder hit districts have given athletic administrators a choice: Find a new way to fund your program or watch it go away" (King 2010, p.15). As a result, reliance upon booster clubs, corporate sponsorships/private partnerships, as well as alumni outreach strategies are all *contemporary dynamics* that will ultimately help interscholastic athletic directors better manage the prospect of cutting sports or consider initiating participation fees.

Managing public perception

When it comes to fundraising, many communities in which interscholastic athletic programs exist have a very strong anti-tax sentiment and therefore, it is imperative that the athletic director and those core booster members clearly communicate the mission and goals of the athletic program and the merits of participation. It is important that messages are well-documented, straightforward and unambiguous, and detail the facts of the fundraising initiative as a *private endeavor* that does not involve the taxation of property or income.

For example, in the neighboring community of Cincinnati Ohio, the Colerain High School Athletic Booster Club raised nearly $500,000 for a field turf project for the school district's football facility. Former Colerain Booster President Greg Stanley indicated, "There were websites out there from groups like COAST, the Coalition Opposed to Additional Spending and Taxes, and we had to contend with those issues and ultimately, it was a significant hurdle we had to overcome not only for this field-turf project, but also for other projects as well such as the press-box, refurbishing the baseball fields etcetera" (Stanley, G. 2009, pers. comm., 25 July). Stanley also referred to the benefits of mail-outs in order to successfully complete the privately funded projects for the Colerain schools: "We mailed out flyers that stated, 'Another project paid in full without taxpayer money! Courtesy of the Colerain Athletic Boosters'" (Stanley, G. 2009, pers. comm., 25 July).

Figure 6.1 A Fundamental Example of Intercollegiate Athletics Revenue

Simultaneously, while there is a strong *anti-tax* sentiment in many communities, in other communities in the United States, there are concerns with *over-commercialization*, regardless of the budget shortfalls among school districts. There is a growing concern that our schools are being perceived and in many cases, *exploited* by corporations as an arena for consumer research. "'U.S. students between 12 and 19 years old have $179 billion in spending power and understand that when brands sponsor an event they know they're being sold something,' said Samantha Skey, executive vice president of strategic marketing for New York-based Alloy Media Marketing" (Cybrzynski 2007, p.1). In the end analysis, each individual school district needs to consider and evaluate the benefits and disadvantages of corporate sponsorships/partnerships. McFarland explains, "It is the responsibility of the athletic director, teachers, coaches and school administration to carefully weigh the benefits of corporate sponsorship with the recognized disadvantages. In other words, it is our responsibility to see the bigger picture" (2002, p.15). Clearly, this aspect of judiciously evaluating the advantages and disadvantages of corporate sponsorships/partnerships is an ethical consideration that must be aligned with the mission of the school district and community at large. Therefore, before entertaining the prospect of partnering with a corporate sponsor, it is vital to truly understand the collective philosophy of the school district and community regarding revenue generation and corporate support. When entering into a school–business relationship, the school, in the end, has the power to negotiate and control the type, size and scope of corporate involvement within the school relative to signage, product placement or even data gathering methodologies for marketing purposes. Pictured on page 88 are specific NBA-type/style scoring tables.

St. Dominic's High School in Oyster Bay, New York and Xaverian High School in Brooklyn, New York benefited as each school received an NBA-type scoring table for free that included eight sponsor-panels from a third-party marketing agency, Sports Image Inc. The school had the *final approval* for content, artwork and scope of involvement. Moreover, after a four-year advertising period, when those sponsorships were renewed by Sports Image Inc., each athletic department generated additional revenue from a new four-year sponsorship signage agreement.

The concepts and strategies are applicable at the youth sport level as well. Pictured on page 88 is a gymnasium wall padding project for a community youth center in Camden, New York. The concept of schools or youth sport organizations utilizing third-party marketing agencies in securing corporate sponsorships will be detailed later in this chapter. The significant line of reasoning to keep in mind here is that if corporate sponsorships/partnerships are carried out judiciously and *controlled* by the athletic administration, this can be a win–win situation for both parties. As was mentioned previously, each individual school district or youth sport organization needs to consider and evaluate the benefits and disadvantages of corporate sponsorships/partnerships. Otherwise, if corporate sponsorships are viewed by the school district administration and community with *corporate exploitation* in mind then perhaps it is best for the athletic director or youth sport administrator to vacate that particular revenue stream and possibly seek out grants applications, and/or alumni outreach strategies for more private support, which will also be detailed in this chapter.

Figure 6.2 NBA-Type Scoring Table: St. Dominic High School, Oyster Bay, NY

Figure 6.3 NBA-Type Scoring Table: Xaverian High School, Brooklyn, NY

Figure 6.4 Gymnasium Wall Padding: Camden, NY

Optimistically, issues such as evaluating the benefits and disadvantages of corporate sponsorships/partnerships need to be well-communicated and understood by all stakeholders of the youth sport organization and/or school system. Moreover, when managing public perception, it is more effective and efficient when all stakeholders strive to focus their energies toward what is best for their most important investment, the *student athletes.*

The importance of good public relations

Concurrent to managing public perception, providing good public relations is a significant piece of the fundraising puzzle. Stier suggests there are five ways to deliver a good public relations program: first, through the actual program itself; second, through personal contact between those involved in the sport program and members of the general public; third, through professional working relationships with representatives of the news media; fourth, through formal public speaking efforts on behalf of those who are a part of the sport program; and last, through actual demonstrations, exhibits, and tangible objects or tools that are seen by the publics (2001, p.96).

For example, as mentioned previously, in their initiative to raise $500,000 for the field turf project at Colerain High School in Cincinnati, Ohio, the booster club had a kickoff rally held at the football stadium that incorporated speeches and testimonials of support by influential coaches, staff, community members and students. Moreover, there were continual press releases placed in the papers that advocated support, and explicitly communicated that no taxpayer money would be used and that the project would be privately funded. Overall, by being *proactive* in providing good, clear, and unambiguous public communication/relations that are well-coordinated, the *attention to detail* regarding those efforts cannot be underestimated and can contribute to fundraising success, as was the case at Colerain High School.

Another aspect regarding booster clubs and the support they exemplify for the athletic programs in their communities is the importance of making sure the booster organization itself has the status of 501(c)(3) tax exemption with the United States Federal Internal Revenue Service, generally referred to as the acronym IRS. While the rules and the bylaws of individual states vary, so do the rules and regulations of the IRS. Further information regarding the determination, instructions and specific forms needed for federal tax exemption can be found at the IRS website at www.irs.gov/index.html. Specific state rules, regulations and forms can be found on state government websites as well. For example, for the State of Ohio, the Ohio Department of Taxation's website is http://www.tax.ohio.gov/index.stm.

Overall, in order to be exempt from income tax, the booster club president and/or their designated representative are responsible for the following: application for 501(c) (3) status; annual filing requirements/time-lines; and public disclosure (if applicable). In the Colerain High School Field Turf project Stanley stated "Having 501(c) (3) status was significant in obtaining our U.S. postal service bulk mail permit. In the end, the bank was offering an eight year loan at five percent interest on $494,000, our goal was to pay it off in five years and we paid it off in 57 months. We sent out an extraordinary amount of mail for this project, which turned out to be a lot of money in postage" (Stanley, G. 2009, pers. comm., 25 July). While there are many perks/ benefits to achieving 501(c) (3) status with the IRS, if your athletic booster club plans to apply for tax-exempt status, the IRS will be looking at your *mission statement* to see if your organization matches its requirements for that type of entity. As a result, all of the work that was accomplished at the outset in crafting a well-documented mission statement will be meticulously reviewed by the IRS.

Cultivating areas of specialty among your fundraising committee

In many instances, this is considered one of the most often overlooked aspects of a successful fundraising initiative. Your committee is the *fundamental key* of your fundraising efforts. Despite the difficulty in recruiting volunteers and quality people to be part of your fundraising initiative, one of the biggest mistakes that can be made is just accepting anyone onto your committee. Therefore, it is best to search for people that are motivated self-starters who can take guidance and direction, yet are also able to function and operate individually. Taking the time to identify their strengths and weaknesses can result in placing the best qualified person in their most appropriate position.

Optimistically, this effort will lead to fundraising success. Moreover, placing people that have particular expertise or *specialty* is just as important. Whether this task is initiated by the Director of Athletics or perhaps delegated to the athletic booster club president, its importance cannot be overestimated.

When dealing with "bricks and mortar" projects, reaching out to and involving people who have specialized skills in areas such as construction management can be a real boon to the design and timeliness of the project. In certain instances, *educators* can get into roles they are either not suited for or that are beyond their qualifications, which can be an obstacle to fundraising and construction management. For example, in California, a gymnasium construction project was compromised when the superintendent of the schools placed a change order in the gymnasium design and as a result, the bleachers stretched beyond the sideline to the three-point line and once extended, the playing area was unsuitable for regulation play. "The bleachers were not part of the original design for the gyms, according to Cornell Williams, the project manager. The seating was added at the request of Pamela Short-Powell, then superintendent of Inglewood Unified School District. Short-Powell had the leverage to amend the original plans, according to Trina Williams, a district board member" (Kyriacou 2010, p.1). Additionally, "Modifying the bleachers would cost between $5 and $6 million, according to an estimate the committee received from the project contractors, FTR International and Icon West, Inc." (Kyriacou 2010, p.1).

In other instances, those who possess the qualifications and expertise on issues related to construction management and key terminology such as *project activities*, *project scheduling* and/or *critical path methodologies* can facilitate the timely procurement of necessary materials, and otherwise insure the completion of a project as soon as possible. In contrast, poor scheduling can result in considerable waste as laborers and equipment wait for the availability of needed resources or the completion of preceding tasks. Furthermore, reaching out to and involving people who have specialized skills and experience with critical path methodologies and allowing them the *autonomy* to help manage projects is a key to success.

In sum, contemporary athletic fundraising activities that are intended to pay for capital construction projects are all about *effective communication* and having the necessary interpersonal skills to know when to pursue, when to back off and listen, when to be aggressive and when to be undemonstrative. Overall, realize that when leading an interscholastic athletic program you're not going to have all of the answers and, as was detailed in Chapter 3, you need to develop *interpersonal competency skills*. Fundamentally, this is exactly why cultivating people who possess areas of specialty among your fundraising committee is so vitally important to fundraising and project success.

IDENTIFYING AND MANAGING *QUID PRO QUO* STRATEGIES

In sports fundraising, you often hear the words *quid pro quo* especially in reference to the making of a gift. At its most basic level, whenever an individual donates to charity they are in fact getting *something for something* and in this case, they are getting a tax deduction for making a gift to a 501(c) (3) or other tax-exempt organization. As was mentioned in Chapter 1, if a donor is receiving a benefit in return (i.e. premium tickets, preferred parking space) for their donation and there is a *quid pro quo*, then there are rules established by the IRS that restrict the donation from being 100 percent tax-deductible. Based on IRS rules, if the donor receives the right to purchase a seat or preferred seating in return for their gift, then only eighty percent of their contribution is tax-deductible. Furthermore, donors should be made aware of this tax rule *prior* to making their donation.

For example, if a donor gives an athletic booster club that has IRS 501(c) (3) status a $100 donation and receives an athletic contest ticket valued at $20, the donor has made a *quid pro quo* contribution. When attempting to identify fundraising activities and the associated *quid pro quo* strategies that go *hand in hand*, it is important to understand that these successful fundraising techniques and strategies on the following pages are intended to inspire action and potential implementation. However, careful consideration needs to be employed based on the particular environmental circumstances as well as the availability of resources, both human and financial. As a result, the fundraising activities and strategies may not be applicable in each and every situation, nor are they intended to be replicated exactly as they are presented. Rather, they are to serve as a model and/or illustration and provide fundraising strategies that are potentially applicable to one's specific circumstances. The idiomatic expression, "there are many ways to skin a cat" can be applied to the various *quid pro quo* strategies being employed by interscholastic athletic booster clubs, as there are many ways to raise money.

The examples presented on the following pages should provide a practical understanding of the fundamental components and general principles of *quid pro quo* strategies and promotional tactics booster clubs utilize. For example, the aforementioned Colerain booster club has an interesting methodology for not only attracting but also retaining members. Figure 6.5 on page 94 is a visual representation of the way in which the Colerain booster club designates the various membership levels and the required amount of money to be donated. The VIP Club program, which includes the five top contribution levels (Platinum, Gold, Silver, Bronze and Varsity Cardinal), includes a VIP-identification badge for the member and spouse. This VIP identification badge allows a fifteen-minute early entry to home football games. Additionally, Stanley points out that "VIP Club members are offered a no waiting concession line at the specially marked window during home football games" (Stanley, G. 2009, pers. comm., 25 July). In addition to the benefits of booster club membership, there are other fundraising activities and *quid pro quo* ideas and strategies utilized by the Colerain Athletic Boosters that are *typical* to the majority of interscholastic athletic programs throughout the United States. The fundraising tactics and activities to follow are by no means original, but are effective and can be modified for the context in which they can be applied. Also, an essential aspect to understand is that the fundraising activities are *ethically appropriate* for the environment/community in which they take place. For example, if within a specific community, they collectively believe that *gambling* is ethically and/or morally objectionable, it makes no sense for an interscholastic athletic program to promote a fundraiser such as a *Texas Hold 'Em Poker Night.* Success in fundraising is a *trial and error* endeavor, but overall, the events and activities that are planned and coordinated should not conflict with the prevailing tenor and/or collective orientation of the community. This is a dynamic of fundraising that cannot be overestimated.

As previously detailed, while one community may frown upon taxes, others may be concerned with over-commercialization and that

Membership Level	1 time Payment	Pay over 5 years	Annual Membership	4 game tickets*	Annual VIP Membership	Stadium Donor Wall*	Fan-wear *	CHS Glassware*	Name on Locker *	CHS Clock*	5 YR. Sports Event Family Pass
Platinum Cardinal - $10,000 ($2,000/ year for 5 years)	Locker Inscription	Locker Inscription									
Gold Cardinal - $5,000 ($1,000.00/ year for 5 years)	Locker Inscription	Locker Inscription									
Silver Cardinal - $2,500 ($500/year for 5 years)	Locker Inscription	Locker Inscription									
Bronze Cardinal - $1000 ($200/year for 5 years)											
Varsity Cardinal - $500 ($100.00/ year for 5 years)											
Red & White Cardinal - $250 ($50/year for 5 years)											
Booster Club - $125											
Individual Locker Purchase (one time donation of $200)											

Figure 6.5 Booster Membership Levels/Perks. Courtesy of the Colerain Booster Club; Cincinnati, OH

regardless of the fundraising activities, *the ends do not justify the means*. This is a significant factor for the athletic director and athletic booster clubs to take into account when choosing their fundraisers. Beyond golf outings, car washes and "split the pot" 50/50 drawings, Stanley states, "Two of our major fundraisers include a reverse raffle and a Monte Carlo night" (Stanley, G. 2009, pers. comm., 25 July). The reverse raffle is an annual event and the boosters generally sell 300 tickets for $100 each. A reverse raffle is a very effective fund-raising activity. 'The advantage of the reverse raffle, in addition to its uniqueness, is that the excitement generated through the awarding of prizes in reverse order is significant. Every ticket purchaser will have his/her ticket actually pulled" (Stanley, G. 2009, pers. comm., 25 July). This style of fundraising creates an intriguing atmosphere and in the case of the Colerain Athletic Boosters, the grand prize is $10,000.

From an observational standpoint, upon comparing fundraising initiatives by parochial schools to those applied among the public schools in the Greater Cincinnati, Ohio area, Stanley (2009, pers. comm., 25 July) suggests "The parochial schools are far more advanced than the public schools are because they have to conduct fundraisers all the time". This viewpoint of the parochial and public schools is considered very *common* among many communities. In fact, local property taxes support the bulk of public education whereas parochial schools do not rely on property taxes, rather they can raise tuition costs, raise significant amounts of money from alumni, and solicit grants from foundations. Consequently, in periods of economic downturn and in communities where there are many voters living on fixed incomes, public schools have been forced to get creative in their fundraising and generate new revenue streams.

As a result, this specific dynamic makes the *fundraising landscape* in many communities across the country even more competitive than it already is. Therefore, the sensible athletic administrator takes this into consideration as an *anticipated challenge* and must develop the skill sets to be creative and resourceful, and to demonstrate a proactive aptitude in working in a united fashion with booster clubs to raise money under these circumstances.

DEVELOPING COOPERATIVE YOUTH SPORT AND INTERSCHOLASTIC PROGRAMS

As was detailed in Chapter 1, the dynamics of fundraising and the ever-increasing competition from other charitable causes are and will continue to be more and more challenging. Additionally, there have been a variety of articles, books, and academic research studies documenting the disturbing trends of inappropriate behavior plaguing youth sports in many communities across the nation. Calls for restoring order and civility in our youth sport programs have been detailed as well. Consequently, there has been an upward trend and a distinctive culture of parents who have their own set of motives and beliefs that youth sport is a "win at all costs" endeavor. The general profile of this group of parents is that they have grown frustrated with community-based sport organizations, because of their organizational structure, and the *rules and guidelines* regarding fair-play, guaranteeing that all children participate and play.

According to NAYS (the National Alliance for Youth Sports), in a report on the status of youth sport in the United States, "The age old notion that children's participation in organized sports should be fun, contribute to physical and emotional development, and enhance social skills has been swept aside in what's become an increasingly hostile environment that's ultra-competitive, high pressured, and often encourages and rewards a do-anything-it-takes-to-win approach" (NAYS 2011, p.13). As a result, these frustrated parents drop out of community-based sport organizations and organize, coach and administer their own versions of youth sports. Many of these youth sport groups foster ultra-competitiveness where all children may practice, but only the best may play in actual game conditions, and the inappropriate behaviors of parents berating referees, coaches, opponents and children are the norm.

Ironically, many of these privately organized youth sport organizations use indoor and outdoor sport/athletic facilities that are school-based and/or community-owned. According to a report by the National Council of Youth Sports or NCYS, they posted a trends and participation report on their website, http://www.ncys.org, that suggests that *all youth sport organizations* used an aggregate of eighty-five percent of outdoor sport facilities and sixty-two percent of indoor sport facilities that are either school-based or community-owned sport facilities in 2008 (NCYS 2011, p.15). From a fundraising perspective, the implication of this data is astonishing. As was previously illustrated in Chapter 1, there is an overwhelming perception that those who use these school-based or publically-owned sports facilities are an extension of the school's local athletics program, which is often wrong and misleading. Therefore, taken a step further, hypothetically, if Johnny's or Suzie's parents are organizing one of these alternative youth sport leagues and as a result, they adopt a "win at all costs" philosophy, the likelihood is that they are using XYZ local school's athletic fields. Consequently, the prevailing perception is that this group is an extension of the XYZ athletic program. Taken to its most logical conclusion, if the youth sport experiences of both children and parents have been indoctrinated in this fashion, a significant portion of the community at large will *think* this is how the program works as a whole.

The negative fallout from this perception can be a public relations nightmare. Furthermore, when it comes to raising funds for support of the athletics and/or youth sport programs, disagreement and lack of support can occur from the community. While *one bad apple doesn't spoil the whole bunch*, it can make enough of a stench to negatively alter the community's perception of your athletic programs and substantially restrain financial support of it. Although it is beyond the scope of this text to address all of the social and psychological issues encompassing youth sports, a fundamental goal is to organize a *symbiotic relationship* with the youth sport groups that are in a community so that ground rules and accountability standards are not only upheld, but also the likelihood of unacceptable behaviors is not tolerated. If these parent-groups who maintain their "win at all costs" philosophy cannot agree with aforementioned rules, they need to find alternative facilities in the private sector. Optimistically, school-based athletic directors and community-based sport program directors need to take the leadership role in communicating and educating youth sport administrators and volunteers about the mission of the athletics program as they are part of the *constituency*.

In conclusion, the majority of youth sport programs that are in the United States are honorable programs and foster appropriate behavior. Notwithstanding, there is a growing need to create alliances and cultivate symbiotic relationships between youth sport organizations and schools-based programs. The key to success in securing external revenue streams and the necessary funds to run a constructive sports program must be through a mission-driven, proactively organized and imaginative group of youth and school-based leaders working together as a team.

CORPORATE SPONSORSHIPS AND THIRD-PARTY MARKETING AGENCIES

As was detailed in Chapter 5, an important view of fundraising to understand is that in the context of an intercollegiate athletic program, fundraising is a *different activity* compared to corporate sponsorships, but the two are *related*. Furthermore, at the intercollegiate level, the intent of corporate sponsorships, which are usually managed by the Sports Marketing and Promotions department, is that there is a mutual agreement between the athletic program and the sponsoring business. As was mentioned in Chapter 1, the size and scope of the organizations themselves relative to their resources, both human and financial, are a significant aspect that *differentiates* intercollegiate and interscholastic athletic programs in regard to fundraising.

The majority of interscholastic athletic programs across the nation are not as *organizationally sophisticated* when compared to intercollegiate athletic departments. At the interscholastic level, most have the administrative oversight of a Director of Athletics and a support staff. However, the main idea to keep in mind is that the inclusion of corporate sponsorships is a *substantial opportunity* for interscholastic athletic departments and/or school districts to capitalize on, to help generate enough revenue to supplement the cost of team and program expenses. Simultaneously, while there has been a gradual alteration of the interscholastic athletic landscape in regard to corporate sponsorships and the concept of advertising in schools since the 1990s, the perpetual decline of public support for our nation's schools has been well-documented and this has forced many administrations to make tough choices in regard to athletics and the inclusion of corporate sponsorships. Some interscholastic athletic programs have been eliminated while others have decided to reach out to corporations and local businesses for support. The situation has evolved to be a *double-edged sword* for both interscholastic athletic administrators as well as school district administrators such as building principals and superintendents. As was mentioned previously, interscholastic athletic departments across the nation lack the resources, both human and financial, to spend the time that is necessary to identify, cultivate and secure corporate sponsorship support compared to their intercollegiate counterparts. Simultaneously, relative to managing public perception, there are those sections within communities that will protest corporate sponsorships because of the concern that our schools are being perceived and/or *exploited* by corporations as an arena for consumer research. Therefore, it's vitally important to reiterate the construct that if the decision has been agreed upon to enter into a school/business relationship, *the school*, in the end, has the power to negotiate and control the type, size and scope of corporate involvement within the school relative to signage, product placement or even data gathering methodologies for marketing purposes.

It is at this stage of the process that, if corporate sponsorships are being considered as an alternative revenue source by an interscholastic athletic program, the *logistics*, of how corporate sponsorship support is to be identified, cultivated and contracted, needs to be carefully and judiciously examined. In general, the human and financial resources of an interscholastic athletic program are stretched so realistic consideration regarding the use of a *third-party marketing agency* needs to be negotiated. The concept of third-party marketing agencies has become quite common in practice among major Division I-A intercollegiate athletic programs over the last fifteen to twenty years. Sneath et al. emphasize "Traditionally, a university athletic department pursues corporate sponsorships through a direct channel of distribution (i.e., the university is in direct contact with potential sponsoring companies). However, this approach to sponsorship requires a large, hard-working staff which can increase costs and take time away from other important duties" (2000, p.1).

In reaction to these issues, third-party intermediaries such as IMG, or International Management Group, in 2007 formed IMG College, which currently holds the licensing rights to over 150 major intercollegiate athletic programs as well as the multimedia marketing rights to many other major Division I-A institutions and conferences, "in effect, acts as a distribution agent, providing efficient and effective channels between these two parties" (Sneath et al. 2000, p.1).

In sum, this approach to securing corporate sponsorships has *trickled down* to the interscholastic athletic level. For example, the mantra of Sports Image Inc. of Miamisburg, Ohio, is "Partnering businesses with schools and organizations to provide equipment and money for youth programs" (Sports Image Inc. 2010, p.1). Cleveland Ohio-based Home Team Marketing is another example of a third-party intermediary that provides marketing partnerships dedicated to the financial support of high school athletics. Marketing intermediaries such as Sports Image Inc. and Home Team Marketing allow interscholastic athletic programs more of an opportunity to use their resources to improve their program from an internal perspective rather than focusing their time and energy on identifying, cultivating and contracting corporate sponsorships. Moreover, this arrangement allows the third-party marketing agency to maximize their already established connections and resources as opposed to the school athletic department organizing staff, coaches and/or boosters who may have relatively no to limited experience in attempting to do the same thing. The fundamental premise to be understood here is that the hiring of a third-party marketing agency could be a feasible option for an interscholastic athletic department, especially since most do not have the human or financial resources needed to secure corporate sponsorships.

Regardless of whether the decision to hire a third-party marketing agency occurs, there are six key areas to understand and appreciate relative to what *motivates* corporations or small businesses in sponsoring athletics at this level. *Reasons* why corporations or small businesses sponsor athletic programs include, but are not limited to, the following:

- *charitable donation*: the company/business has a certain amount of money earmarked for worthwhile causes and this is a prospective tax write-off with the IRS.
- *strategic philanthropy*: this involves the dual aims of targeting both business objectives and recipient needs.
- *ego enhancement*: names and reputations are valuable and the sponsor is ultimately interested in advancing his or her recognition within the community.
- *linkage to the school*: perhaps the sponsor is an alumnus or their children/grandchildren attend or attended that school.
- *straightforward advertising*: this involves promoting and generating increased sales or foot traffic for sponsor products or services.
- *staying ahead of the competition*: by sponsoring an interscholastic athletic program, they value sponsorship exclusivity. Overall, they want to be the only sponsor in their product category and do not want their competition involved.

As previously stated, the majority of interscholastic athletic departments across the nation lack the resources to spend the time and money that are necessary to identify, cultivate and secure corporate sponsorships. The actual time it takes to network through the minutia of people and ultimately get in front of an actual *decision-maker* is in many cases very burdensome. Additionally, the time and resources needed to accomplish this task from start to finish mean that most high school athletic departments and their booster clubs lack the resources to do the job effectively.

The consideration and potential inclusion of corporate sponsorships is a *substantial opportunity* for these athletic departments and/or school districts to capitalize on and based on the lack of resources, a third-party marketing agency could be a feasible option.

In conclusion, there are a variety of challenges that will continually test the athletic director's creativity, tenacity and entrepreneurial spirit. Therefore, creativity and the aggressive pursuit of alternative funding sources, such as corporate sponsorships, are not merely desirable, but imperative for the majority of interscholastic athletic departments across the United States.

ALUMNI OUTREACH STRATEGIES

A key component to fundraising efforts at both the intercollegiate and interscholastic athletic levels involves the role of *alumni relations.* There have been empirical studies that substantiate a positive correlation between the degree of alumni involvement and the level of their financial backing to the school. "Alumni who are interested, concerned, and involved not only are a good source for substantial dollars, but they also can be instrumental in securing dollars from corporations, foundations, friends of the institution, and other sources" (Webb 2002, p.333). For example, Massachusetts Institute of Technology produced some insightful results by measuring the relationship between the degree of alumni involvement with the level of their financial backing.

"The findings were stunning: Regardless of graduating class, department, or current geographic location, alumni who were 'involved in MIT alumni activities' gave 'much more frequently than their uninvolved peers'" (Webb 2002, p.333). This study provides insightful information that athletic departments and/or booster clubs can utilize when planning for fundraisers. Moreover, the study at MIT "found that merely attending class reunions or centennial activities was as significant a factor as actual volunteer activity – if not more so" (Webb 2002, p.334). At the interscholastic level, this is substantial information to be incorporated into wisely planned alumni outreach strategies. A focal point here is the concept of *recognition*. The following strategies are in no order of importance, but should be considered as a *game plan* for connecting and re-connecting with alumni and the provision of appropriate recognition:

- Make a concerted effort to reach out and work with individuals associated with school alumni affairs or with class representatives in networking/coordinating athletic events with class reunions.
- Work with student leadership groups (e.g. Student Council members) who can help in promoting, leveraging and/or engaging alumni and increase attendance at home events.
- Try to improve communications and regularity with alumni through the use of *offline methods* such as physical newsletters, physical press-releases, postcards with event announcements, etc., in addition to *online methods* such as e-newsletters, e-mail announcements, and social networking (i.e. Facebook, Twitter, MySpace).
- Identify a strategic series of special events, such as dinners, social receptions, golf tournaments or some other creative alumni-centered hospitality.
- Implement an *Alumni Appreciation Day* in addition to or in conjunction with *homecoming* for all sports and activities with specialized recognition for former student athletes, former

Figure 6.6 Alumni Appreciation Photo, courtesy of the Colerain High School Boosters, Cincinnati, OH

band-members, and other key alumni who were or are connected to the athletic program.

There is reliable research in addition to the MIT study that demonstrates "These studies, and others conducted across the country, provide incontrovertible evidence that alumni involvement in meaningful alumni activities correlates directly with the size and frequency of gifts" (Webb 2002, p.335). Therefore, the importance of actively engaging school alumni through the previously mentioned strategies is a key component to the ultimate success of fundraising initiatives implemented by interscholastic athletic programs.

The overall importance of athletic fundraising and relationship cultivation/stewardship among the interscholastic athletic fundraising discipline cannot be overemphasized. There are a wide variety of contemporary dynamics that interscholastic athletic programs face, especially in periods of economic downturn. Compounded with the reality that many people in communities across the nation live on fixed incomes, public schools in particular have been forced to get creative in their fundraising ideas and come up with strategies to generate new revenue streams.

In many instances across the United States, this reality has forced many educational and athletic administrations to make some tough choices, for example, the decision to cut athletic programs or to initiate participation or "pay to play" fees. Consequently, this has led many programs across the nation to consider the financial support of corporations through sponsorship arrangements. Cultivating and securing corporate sponsorship money is not an easy task and takes a significant amount of time and resources. Many well-intentioned school athletic department staff, coaches, and/or boosters can assist in reaching out to potential corporate sponsors, however, when it comes to understanding the dynamic nature of obtaining corporate sponsorships, interscholastic athletic departments and their stakeholders either have relatively no or limited experience, or they don't have the required time to do it because they have other full-time jobs or commitments.

In conclusion, connecting with non-donors and getting them involved is of major concern among colleges and universities. Athletic fundraisers need to communicate the giving process more effectively and consistently. Also, athletic fundraisers need to clearly demonstrate to non-donors exactly where their gifts would go, who it would help and explain that their financial participation can make a difference. In general, giving decisions are varied and in many instances, irrational. Therefore, there needs to be an emphasis on leveraging emotional appeals in addition to the impersonal approaches. In other words, a sensible balance between physical mailings and personalized telephone solicitations appeals needs to be tracked and recorded. These are lessons that are applicable to all levels, college, youth and high school. The prudent athletic fundraiser, regardless of the level they are managing, must develop the skill sets to be creative, resourceful and a dynamic leader in working closely with booster clubs.

Simultaneously, they must recognize the merits of third-party marketing intermediaries and interpersonal skills to provide proper recognition to alumni groups, in order to raise significant amounts of money. These are not merely desirable skill sets, but imperative for the contemporary athletic administrator to possess.

FURTHER READING

Baade, R. A. and Sundberg, J. O. (1996) "Fourth down and goal to go? Assessing the link between athletics and alumni giving", *Social Science Quarterly*, 77 (4) 789–803.

Bravo, G. A. (2004) "An investigation of stakeholder influence and institutional pressures on budget strategies of high school athletic departments", Ohio State University, available at http://search.proquest.com/docview/305139790?accountid=2909 (accessed 01/31/12).

Browder, B. R. (2007) "Commercialism in public schools: A study of the perceptions of superintendents accepting corporate advertising in Virginia", Virginia Polytechnic Institute and State University, available at http://search.proquest.com/docview/304790638?accountid=2909 (accessed 01/31/12).

Burden, W. and Li, M. (2003) "Differentiation of NCAA Division I Athletic Departments in outsourcing of sport marketing operations: A discriminant analysis of financial-related institutional variables", *International Sports Journal*, 7 (2) 74–81.

Coughlin, C. C. and Erekson, O. H. (1984) "Contributions to intercollegiate athletic programs: Further evidence", *Social Science Quarterly*, 194–202.

Driscoll, G. J. (2004) "An analysis of the working relationships between in-house and outsources sports marketing departments in division I-A college athletics", University of North Carolina-Chapel Hill, available at http://search.proquest.com/docview/305286616?accountid=2909 (accessed 01/31/12).

James, R. N. (2008) "Distinctive characteristics of educational donors", *International Journal of Educational Advancement*, 8 (1) 3–13.

Kelleher, L. A. (2011) "Alumni participation: An investigation using relationship marketing principles", University of Nevada, Las Vegas, available at http://search.proquest.com/docview/879040514?accountid=2909 (accessed 01/31/12).

McFarland, A. J. (2002) "'What's in It for Us?' Rethinking Corporate Sponsorships in Interscholastic Athletics", Education Resources Information Center (ERIC) document (ED465738), available at http://www.eric.ed.gov/PDFS/ED465738.pdf (accessed 01/31/12).

Merkel, R. E. (2010) "Managing the relationship between the student and the university, a case study in the context of development and alumni relations", University of Maryland, available at http://search.proquest.com/docview/648974611?accountid=2909 (accessed 01/31/12).

Smith, S. J. (2001) "An investigation of athletic participation fee practices in Ohio public high schools", University of Missouri-Columbia, available at http://search.proquest.com/docview/304706723?accountid=2909 (accessed 01/31/12).

Tomasini, N., Frye, C. and Stotlar, D. K. (2004) "NCAA corporate sponsor objectives: Are there differences between divisions I-A, I-AA, and I-AAA?" *Sport Marketing Quarterly*, 13 (4).

Tucker, I. B. (2004) "A reexamination of the effect of big-time football and basketball success on graduation rates and alumni giving", *Economics of Education Review*, 23 (6) 655–661.

Weight, E., Taylor, K. and Cuneen, J. (2010) "Corporate Motives for Sport Sponsorship at Mid-Major Collegiate Athletic Departments", *Journal of Issues in Intercollegiate Athletics*, 119–130.

Worth, M. J. (2002) *New strategies for educational fundraising*, Westport, CT: American Council on Education and Praeger Publishers.

APPLICATION/SKILL BUILDING EXERCISE

Exercise 1: for students

Select a college or high school of your choice to examine/study. Get on the Internet and browse the school's website. Most public or parochial schools have a website, and in many instances the athletic department's website/web page is separate from the institution's so you may need to browse a separate link to view it. Based on the chapter lessons regarding *booster clubs*, *corporate sponsorships* and *third-party marketing intermediaries* as well as *alumni outreach strategies*, try to answer the following questions:

- Does the athletic department of the high school you chose to examine have their booster club information posted or is there a link to the booster club's website?
- If so, does the booster club provide any detailed information if they are a 501(c) (3) not-for-profit organization? If not, does the booster club provide any detailed information on membership (e.g. benefits chart); the fundraising activities they are promoting or perhaps a detailed list of their corporate partners?

Based on the information you gathered (even if there was no booster information listed) and taking into consideration what you have just learned in reading this chapter, reflect and answer the following question:

- What were the relative strengths and weaknesses of the athletic booster club's website? If you were to change/modify it, identify and explain why you would change and/or modify the areas you chose. If there wasn't one; identify and explain the areas you would consider incorporating if there was one.

Attempt to contact the Director of Athletics at a high school of your choice. Try to coordinate a face-to-face interview or perhaps a phone interview based on his/her availability/schedule. Relative to the chapter lesson on corporate sponsorships and third-party marketing intermediaries, engage the Director of Athletics to answer questions *you create* among the following areas:

- the athletic director's perception as to the community's sentiment toward school-based taxes
- the athletic director's perception as to the feasibility of corporate sponsorships as an alternative revenue source
- the athletic director's perception as to the resources of his/her athletic department and whether or not hiring a third-party marketing agency would merit consideration
- the athletic director's perception of the type and frequency of alumni outreach strategies utilized by the department and/or the booster club.

Exercise 2: for practitioners

Based on the chapter lessons regarding *youth sports*, *corporate sponsorships* and *third-party marketing intermediaries* as well as *alumni outreach strategies*, try to answer the following questions:

- What is your stance as to the feasibility of *corporate partnerships* as an alternative revenue source? Would the school/community at large support it or snub the idea citing issues with over-commercialization or corporate exploitation? If supported, would the resources of your athletic department be sufficient to create/maintain corporate partnerships or would the hiring of a third-party marketing agency need to be considered?
- What is the sentiment of your community toward school-based taxes?
- How many youth sport organizations utilize your athletic facilities?
- How important are public relations to you and how would you go about ensuring that the philosophic missions of the youth sport organizations that play in your facilities are aligned with the mission of your athletic program?
- Is there a philosophic disconnect between the organizations?
- To what extent does the community think that the youth sports played in your athletic facilities reflect your mission/objectives?
- What is the relationship you have with the youth sport administrators who use your facilities?
- What kind of alumni outreach strategies are utilized by the department and/or the booster club (i.e. dinners, social receptions, golf

tournaments, homecoming events or some other creative alumni-centered hospitality)?

- What communication outlets do you use to promote them: newspaper, radio/television, online methods, physical mailings?
- What are some other resources you utilize in reaching out to and re-connecting with alumni?

CHAPTER 7

LEVERAGING POINTS OF SALE AND PROFIT-MAKING FOR FUNDRAISING SUCCESS

The intent of this chapter is to identify and explain the significant elements, principles and methods of profit-making strategies in sports fundraising among the intercollegiate, youth and interscholastic levels. Another aim is to examine the common elements between college and youth sport/interscholastic athletics and to establish if there are any aspects of college points of sale, profit-making principles/methodologies that can potentially be incorporated at the youth/ interscholastic levels. Finally, the ways in which maximizing points of sale affects fundraising will also be explained.

In a general sense, "points of sale" refers to the *location* where a product or service can be purchased. Also known as "POS", this term is commonly associated with the retail industry, and involves the *place of transaction between a buyer and a seller.* For example, a typical point of sale involves a physical location, such as buying popcorn or a slice of pizza at a concession stand at a sports facility. A different point of sale may involve a *virtual location*, where the transaction takes place via a website on the Internet, for example, the purchase of a football jersey or other type of licensed merchandise on a school's website or on the website of a sporting goods manufacturer. This concept has been thoroughly developed and has been a significant revenue stream for many intercollegiate athletic programs across the nation. By and large, creating awareness and promoting the merits of attendance are essential to attracting people to games and events, who in turn, consume food, beverages and have the opportunity to buy licensed merchandise. Primarily, this chapter will focus on the following points of sale:

- ticket sales
- concession sales
- licensed merchandise sales.

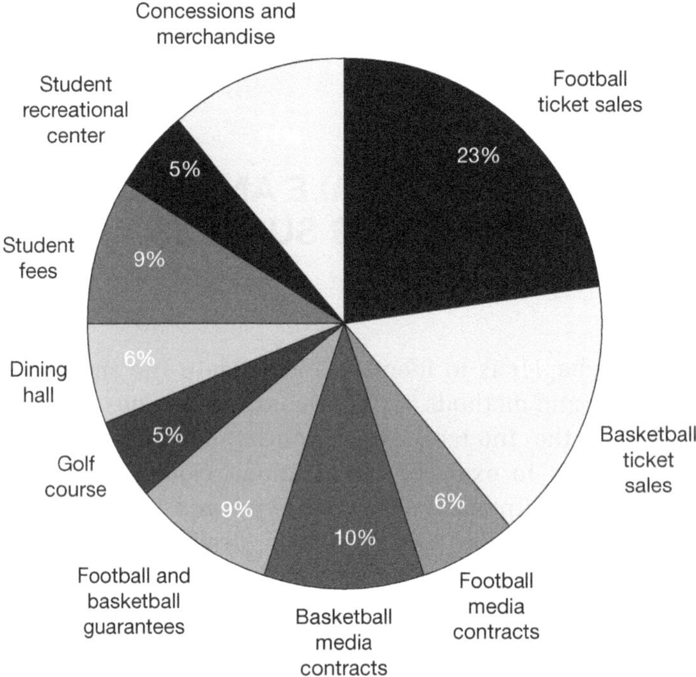

Figure 7.1 Intercollegiate Athletics Income/Revenues Budget

ATTENDANCE AND TICKET SALE REVENUE

Attendance at sporting events is a definitive *key driver* for the money-making potential among ticket sales, concession sales and licensed merchandise sales. Consequently, at the forefront of increasing attendance is through *ticket sales revenue*, because ticket sales drive all of the other revenue streams previously mentioned. Figure 7.1 is a fundamental example of the income/revenues of an intercollegiate athletic department. While there are separate ancillary activities that generate a profit for an athletic program, such as game/event program sales, vending machines and parking fees (if applicable), in general, ticket sales, concession sales and licensed merchandise sales are the primary areas that have the greatest potential for positive cash flow during an athletic event.

In the hypothetical example on page 110, the combination of ticket sales, concession sales and merchandise income is equal to fifty percent of the entire income/revenues. The essential factor to keep in mind is that the percentages will vary from one athletic department to another. However, the reality is that these three areas, based on attendance, are the crucial elements for cash flow/revenue generation. Moreover, what will be discussed later in this chapter is the way that the most significant growth area for raising brand awareness and revenue is through the management of a licensed merchandising program and in particular, how youth and interscholastic athletic programs can benefit financially from the sale of licensed merchandise.

The primary theme of this book has been the reality of the financial challenges faced among all youth and school-based athletic programs in the United States and how expenses have outpaced revenues. Specifically, there is an NCAA report on revenues and expenses among Division I Intercollegiate Athletic Programs ranging from 2004–2008. In this particular study, there were three groups that were surveyed: the Football Bowl Subdivision schools (formerly referred to as Division I-A); the Football Championship Subdivision (formerly referred to as Division I-AA); and Division I without football (formerly referred to as Division I-AAA). Among all three groups that were examined, "In all subdivisions, three revenue sources account for well over fifty percent of total generated revenues. These are Ticket Sales, Alumni and Booster Contributions, and NCAA and Conference Distributions" (NCAA 2008, p.8). It is evident, therefore, that *ticket sales* are a key element and a significant piece of the pie for the Division-I Intercollegiate Athletic Programs.

Additionally, there are a number of approaches to increasing ticket sales revenue that also allow for a significant return on investment and cost efficiency. From a contemporary standpoint, the marketing and promotion of tickets among intercollegiate athletics through *social media*, particularly *social networking sites*, has become significant in terms of efficient customer service and cost-effectiveness. It allows you to reach your fan base very quickly and it is economically practical. Steinbach writes, "Ticket sales represent the overwhelming majority of revenue generation in most college athletic departments, and the potential impact of social media on ticket marketing is limited only by the imagination" (2010, p.1). For example, in 2008, the University of Utah's football team had more than 500 season tickets left to sell. Within two hours of posting the information on the Utah Athletics' Facebook page, the remaining season tickets sold out. The use of social media sites such as Facebook and/or Twitter in intercollegiate athletics also means there is less cost put into advertising, and the messages reach your intended audience much quicker than writing press releases to the traditional media outlets such as newspapers or radio stations. According to the University of Utah's Assistant Athletics Director for Corporate Sales and Operations, Zach Lassiter, "There are people we know are specifically opting in and asking for information about our programs. To not service these people in this way would be silly" (Steinbach 2010, p.1). Therefore, as social media grows, it's clearly an area that has great potential in increasing ticket-sale revenue. Technology continually evolves and in many cases, redefines how people interact and network with one another and as such, the use of social media is clearly an emerging technology that has only *scratched the surface* in terms of its impact on both the intercollegiate and youth/interscholastic athletic domains.

An additional challenge for athletic programs in increasing ticket sales is the somewhat elusive and arbitrary concept of *pricing strategies*. External factors affecting attendance figures such as the economy, increased competition from other industries such as the video game industry, the film/movie industry and cable and satellite television expansion, have all played a significant role in how pricing strategies are considered. Many big-time athletic institutions including the aforementioned Football Bowl Subdivision schools, "have developed 'priority seating' programs for football, which ties preferred seating locations to additional donations to the athletic program" (Howard and Crompton 2004, p.355). In other words, in order to get the best seats within the stadium, people could pay up to as much as $5000 for the *right* to purchase a single season ticket from a major Football Bowl Subdivision school. A *personal seat license*, or PSL, gives the holder the right to buy season tickets for a certain seat in a stadium. This holder can sell the seat license to someone else if they no longer wish to purchase season tickets. It is an *upfront fee* before being able to purchase season tickets. As the old idiom goes, "you reap what you sow": the larger the donation is to the school's athletic department, the better the location of the seat. Despite the fact that the majority of the Football Bowl Subdivision schools utilize the priority seating concept, the tricky or arbitrary part of this is determining the price of tickets and the rights fee.

"Research has shown that consumers have an expected range of prices that they are willing to pay for a particular program or service and for various products" (Howard and Crompton 2004, p.357). As a result, many athletic programs have created their own misfortune by incorporating the notion of charging people *what the market will bear*. However, while it may produce desirable monetary results in the short term, this concept can prove costly in the long term. Take for example the ever-present *ticket scalper* for a high-demand college athletic event. Ticket scalpers can charge in excess of 200–300 percent higher than the face value of the price printed on the ticket. For those people who don't have a ticket, there is no previous or existing business relationship between them and the ticket scalper. Therefore, once the transaction is over and a person pays $200 on a $25 dollar ticket, chances are, they will never do business with the ticket scalper again.

Now let's assume the same scenario, except that same person walks up to the ticket booth at the stadium, where there has been a previous and existing business relationship between the athletic ticket office and the customer. Hypothetically suppose that the game is between two conference rivals and demand for tickets is high. As a result, the ticket office decides to charge $50 on the same $25 dollar ticket, or a 100 percent rise in ticket price. Even though there is the potential to make a large profit by the ticket office, the core concern for the ticket office is to *repeat business*. Whilst repeat business is not very high on the priority list of a ticket scalper, it is the lifeblood for the ticket office. When coming up with a pricing strategy, an intelligent procedure would be by *differentiating* the long-term trends of your fan base/season ticket holders with the changes of short-term supply/demand of tickets. Moreover, making a *quick buck* can prove costly because repeat business is the key to success in ticket sales, especially at a time when the economy is sluggish. Therefore, many schools and universities have utilized pricing strategies that do take into account the long-term trends with the short-term supply and demand of tickets called *variable pricing*. For instance, at the University of Miami in Coral Gables, Florida, they have tracked and recorded the data of ticket sales over a twenty-year period in order to help determine the price of future games. In fact, back in 2002, it was decided that "The school will charge $45 for its home games against Florida State and Virginia Tech, $40 against Pittsburgh and Boston College and $35 against the University of Connecticut and Florida A & M" (Rowell

2002, p.3). The concept here is that the price will be determined to be higher for games that have a history of a significantly large attendance and demand for tickets than those that don't.

According to Patrick Nero, who was the Senior Associate Athletic Director at Miami back in 2002, "It's the fans who are deciding that a Miami–Florida State game is more important than a Miami–McNeese State game" (Rowell 2002, p.3). Thus, variable pricing has been used as a successful pricing strategy at the University of Miami by understanding that natural rivalries, like the one that exists between Florida State and Miami, as well as other significant rivalries, can have a significant impact on raw sales income. "Since both Florida State and the Virginia Tech games sold out when the two schools visited two years ago, Miami raised the price of both games by $5, which Nero says will bring in an additional $800,000 in gross revenue" (Rowell 2002, p.3). While this type of strategy may work in Miami, perhaps it may be perceived as a type of *price gouging* by a community in a different part of the country.

Other types of ticket pricing strategies involve promotional giveaways such as bobble-heads, ball-caps with team logos, fleece stadium blankets with team logos etc., while others utilize the concept of mini-season ticket plans and/or mini-game packages that incorporate different options in order to help drive increases in attendance. For example, a mini-season ticket plan usually involves the pre-sale of a specified number of less popular opponents as well as at least one natural rivalry or high-demand opponent, and is significantly less expensive than an entire season ticket package.

Regardless of the pricing strategy that is used, there needs to be an *effective communication plan* with your stakeholders, who are your current season ticket holders. Perhaps sending out a survey to current season ticket holders which ask questions such as "what kind of season ticket benefits do we offer?" or "what did you like about your experience?" or questions geared to assess what they would like to see changed will help in servicing the customer as well as aid in increasing future attendance. The final ticket pricing strategy, but certainly not the least in terms of importance, is through the concept of special discounted rate tickets as well as the use of complimentary/free tickets.

Research has demonstrated that tickets at a special discounted rate can influence people to attend sporting events and is a technique that has proven to be effective at the professional and intercollegiate level. Additionally, "This technique might also have similar, practical results at the high school level" (Stier 2001, p.178). There are a variety of tactics to consider when *incentivizing* fans/spectators to support and attend athletic events. Specific examples of how to do this with special discounted rate tickets include, but are not limited to, the following:

- discounted/reduced price tickets for specialized groups within the community, such as Boy/Girl Scout Troops, other local youth groups, members of community service or charitable organizations such as the Elks Club or Lions Club International, local VFW-Veterans of Foreign Wars of the United States, etc.
- special promotional events, with offers such as "wear your school's logo on a T-shirt/jacket/sweatshirt and get a half-price admission ticket", "wear your favorite team's ball cap and get a discounted rate ticket", "wear a pink T-shirt/jacket/sweatshirt to support breast cancer awareness and get a discounted rate ticket", etc.
- sponsor-related events: discounted tickets upon the presentation of a merchant membership card, such as Sam's Club, Costco, Kroger's, an AAA Driver card, or employee ID of a local hospital, financial institution, supermarket, or from a sponsoring business or some other merchant that is affiliated with or a corporate sponsor of your athletic department
- complimentary/free ticket giveaways to, for example, local elementary/middle-junior high schools, local YMCA/YWCAs, local Boys/Girls Club of America, local senior assisted living centers, etc.
- BOGOF (buy one, get one free) campaigns, or offers such as "purchase two tickets get the third ticket free", "purchase three and get the fourth ticket free", etc.

The benefits of this pricing strategy are threefold:

1. It directly increases attendance;
2. It has the potential to fill the athletic facility to near capacity;
3. It simultaneously draws support from loyal fans and cultivates new spectators.

Overall, whatever pricing strategy that is utilized by the athletic program at either level, the key to success includes the following components:

- driving repeat business
- having an effective communications plan with season ticket holders
- utilizing tactics that increase attendance
- attempting to fill the facility to capacity
- elicit support of loyal fans and cultivate new spectators.

Utilizing these strategies can significantly draw more business to the ancillary points of sale, such as the concession stands and the licensed merchandise kiosks.

THE CONCESSIONS INDUSTRY

From an operational standpoint, concessions among intercollegiate or even interscholastic athletic events have experienced a dramatic *paradigm shift*. What was once a generally accepted ancillary activity of boxing popcorn, grilling and/or boiling hot dogs and pouring soda pop into cups has incrementally evolved into revenue- and technology-driven procedures coupled with a focus on customer service.

Although there are many intercollegiate athletic programs across the nation that have *in-house* concession operations, in recent years there has been an incremental shift away from this practice. Outsourcing concession operations is happening more and more on many campuses nationwide. Ammon, Southall and Blair state, "An efficiently managed concession operation plays a vital role in the financial success of any facility". Furthermore, "Game day revenue at major college football games can amount to as much as $350,000" (2003, p.192).

Upon examining the revenue potential of concessions, there also needs to be careful consideration of the time, money and resources it takes to undertake a successful concession operation. Therefore, *planning* is a significant aspect. The ultimate goal is to provide low cost food and beverages that will net a high profit with a relatively low amount of work and a high level of customer service. Overall, from a business or profit-making perspective, a successful concession operation is determined when there is a large enough profit that can be realized at the end of the day. Simultaneously, a successful concession operation requires a *customer service focused orientation* so that fans and patrons who consume the products are satisfied that the quality of food, service and price are meeting or exceeding their expectations. Stier comments on this, stating "This means that the profit margins (money remaining after cost of sales and merchandise is deducted) must be high enough to warrant the involvement (time and effort) in concessions" (2001, p.178). Additionally, having a concession operation that is focused on customer service in addition to profit-making will help foster long-term success. Athletic organizations that are genuinely interested in increasing the profitability of the concessions operation need to be mindful of these dual aspects.

"Obviously long lines, cold food, warm beer, or dirty conditions will cause customers to refrain from making purchases, but other issues such as customer service and employee appearance also affect overall sales" (Ammon, Southall and Blair 2003, p.193). Therefore, planning for and creating an operation that is both high in quality and aesthetically pleasing need to be significant priorities if this is a revenue stream that is to be potentially maximized. In the end, this can be an expensive undertaking. For many intercollegiate athletic programs, the decisions to outsource their concession operations are, in many instances, based on the following criteria. First and foremost is the cost of the product(s) and operations. The amount of money needed to operate a successfully efficient and effective concession operation relative to the time and resources (financial and human), is quite considerable, especially among the Football Bowl Subdivision Schools. At the University of Florida, the average per game revenue from concessions is $164,357, whilst the total for a seven home game season equals $1,150,500 (SportsBusiness Journal Daily Article 2009). At the University of Michigan, the athletics department "generated $3.2 million in gross food revenue at all sports facilities, $2.5 million alone from Michigan Stadium (Muret 2010, p.1). Some of the sport facility concessionaire industry leaders include Aramark, Delaware North Companies, Centerplate, and Sodexo, just to name a few. In fact, Sodexo, as of 2010, contracted with the University of Michigan to operate the "general concessions and premium dining at Michigan Stadium, Crisler Arena, Yost Ice Arena and several other sports venues on campus" (Muret 2010, p.1) which should benefit the athletic department significantly as a key revenue stream. Issues and dynamics relative to staffing, inventory, product, storage, equipment etc. shifts away from the school to the outsourced company, as well as risk/liability issues related to workman's compensation, hiring/firing decisions, and food quality issues. Financially, outsourcing usually profits the athletic department "anywhere from 25–50% profit, depending upon variables such as facility size, type of facility, and length of contract" (Ammon, Southall and Blair 2003, p.194).

The gradual change away from in-house concessions to companies like Aramark and Sodexo is a contemporary dynamic that has evolved over the last two decades and is a significant paradigm shift within the intercollegiate athletic landscape. It has the potential to have an eventual impact on interscholastic athletics as well. Traditionally, the majority of high school athletic programs have, at the very least, one centralized location for concession sales. For the most part, the organizational and operational dynamics of high school athletic concessions typically involves a combination of separate booster groups (i.e. band booster parents, or the baseball boosters or the soccer boosters) that, for the most part, do not generate a large attendance. Moreover, they will typically volunteer their time to operate the concessions at the home football and/or basketball game for a pre-determined percentage of the net sales. In some instances, an efficiently organized and operated concession setup has allowed some non-revenue sports teams, boosters and/or band booster clubs to gain revenue ranging from $15,000 to $25,000 from the combined football and basketball seasons.

For illustration purposes, Figure 7.2 on page 119 is a generalized example of this concept. It shows, for instance, that the Band Boosters at the *Unified School* operated the concession stand for one boys' basketball game and brought in $500 in concession sales that evening. The cost of the items/products sold (i.e. the popcorn, hot dogs, candy, beverages etc.) equaled $159 and the sales tax was 8%. Therefore, once those were deducted from the total revenues provided the actual profit made by the concession stand equaled $301. As a result, the share of the Band Boosters in this example equals 80% of the profit or $240.80, whilst the Unified Athletic Booster Club General Fund receives 20% of the profit or $60.20.

Clearly the cost of products and the sales tax can vary from one athletic concession operation to the next, but the key concept to understand

Total revenues: $500.00
Less:
Sales tax (8%) (–$40.00)
Cost of items sold (–$159.00)
Total cost: $159.00 (–$199.00)
Profit $301.00
Band booster share (80% of profit) $240.80
Unified school's athletic booster club general fund share (20% of profit) $60.20

Figure 7.2 Concession Sales Example at Boys' Basketball Game, Unified Athletic Boosters Club

here is that the benefits of this arrangement are two-fold. First, it provides those specific programs that are considered *non-revenue* sports or extracurricular activities an opportunity to raise revenue for their individual sport and/or activity. Secondly, it provides an additional opportunity to advance the general fund with a pre-arranged percentage of overall sales. In the previous example, the band is the primary beneficiary of the funds ($240.80) and the athletic general fund benefits as well ($60.20). As was stated in Chapter 2, while certain stakeholders may cite that having separate clubs is the way things have been done from a historical/traditional perspective, diplomatically working towards and implementing a uniform as well as unified booster club is ultimately the *best practice.*

When concession sales and operations are at the forefront of conversations among boosters/stakeholders of the athletic program, the Director of Athletics, regardless of whether the organizations are unified as one or if they are divided among a variety of sports and activities, must *communicate* that the vital aim of the boosters is to support all sport teams, activities and programs. In the end, booster club(s) must be properly educated that their function is to support the entire program by enhancing the school spirit through positive role modeling, promoting good sportsmanship and overall moral support. Stier sums up the responsibility of the athletic director's role as "to seek to *create* ideas and concepts, to *initiate* actions, to *cultivate, titillate,* and *motivate* others as well as to *educate* constituencies so that athletic programs might *captivate* their interests and loyalties and thus *facilitate* the *solicitation* of both tangible (concrete) and intangible (moral) support" (Stier 2001, p.235). In other words, while there are financial and human resource limitations beyond the control of the high school athletics director, they can control the quality and frequency of their relations with the stakeholders of the athletic program.

INTELLECTUAL PROPERTY AND LICENSED MERCHANDISING PROGRAMS

The concept of licensed merchandising in intercollegiate athletics has grown dramatically over the last three decades and the amount of revenue it produces is quite significant. Fundamentally, there are three primary objectives relative to *licensing* (often referred to as *intellectual property*) and the importance of these objectives cannot be overemphasized. The purposes of a licensed merchandise program are to protect, promote and generate profit. "Licensing brings in revenue and generates publicity and exposure. It results in walking billboards with people paying you to carry your advertising message" (Revoyr 1995, p.2).

While the licensing of trademarks, logos and other intellectual property of various intercollegiate athletic programs have proven to be a significant revenue stream, high school athletic programs, until recently, have not benefited. In many instances across the nation, the production and sale of *unlicensed merchandise* has occurred in many nationally known retail department store chains. Addressing the growing popularity in high school sports and the issues related to unlicensed merchandise in the marketplace, in 2009 the National Federation of State High School Associations (NFHS) along with the Licensing Resource Group, LLC (LRG) initiated a nationwide licensing program, which will be detailed later in the chapter.

There are dual objectives of this section of the chapter. While there are many significant and detailed aspects of the *licensing process* that are beyond the scope of this text, a fundamental overview of the key elements is essential. The first objective is to explain the fundamental purpose of successful licensed merchandise programs, and the three "P"s: protect, promote and profit (Revoyr 1995); second is to identify and explain the issues related to the calculation and management of royalty. The emphasis of this section of the text is to highlight the importance of licensed merchandise as a revenue stream and how to go about using a licensing program to maximize exposure in the marketplace. Issues related to unauthorized use of mascots, logos and other trademarks or color schemes associated with the institution will also be addressed.

Licensing can be defined as the process where the owner (the *licensor*) of a trademark, trade name, logo, or other type of intellectual property such as a school's color scheme, grants permission through a legal agreement for a company (the *licensee*), to produce and distribute goods and services with those marks and/or colors.

The protection aspect of licensing has a dual purpose. The first aspect is to protect the image, reputation and credibility of the school/institution by preventing *infringers* making a profit off of their name, logo or other type of intellectual property. Secondly, a licensing program protects consumers from deception. This is a *fundamental prerequisite* of licensing. Revoyr states, "Since a trademark is supposed to protect consumers from deception regarding the source and quality of the product or service bearing the mark, according to the legal theory, the licensor has the legal responsibility of controlling the quality of goods and services offered by the licensee bearing the licensed marks" (1995, p.17). Without this element or the effective enforcement of it, there is relatively no opportunity to promote the merits of the institution nor profit from it either. A key component to this concept of *protection from deception* is through the use of hangtags or "hologram stickers" on licensed merchandise. This measure provides consumers the ability to identify authentic and/or "officially" licensed merchandise. Consequently, "In each case, a product that doesn't have this hangtag or sticker is very likely to be counterfeit" (Irwin, Sutton and McCarthy 2002, p.262). The following paragraph is a good example concerning the concept of protection and as such, explains the responsibilities of the University of Cincinnati's Office of Trademarks and Licensing:

> The University of Cincinnati Board of Trustees has established a licensing program to protect the name and identifying marks of the university and to prohibit the unauthorized use of university marks on commercial or other products. In addition, in order to comply with and assure protection under federal, state,

> and international trademark laws, the University of Cincinnati is required to monitor and control all uses of its trademarks. Unauthorized use of UC trademarks is subject to civil and criminal penalties. The university reserves the right to take appropriate action when confronted with unauthorized use of its trademarks. Such actions may include confiscation of the goods, financial penalties, and legal action.
>
> (Trademarks and Licensing General Information, n.d., p.1)

In other instances, there are *unlicensed products* being produced bearing the name, mascot and/or logos of high schools across the United States. Many schools are being exploited, consumers are being misled and in the end, the schools don't gain any financial benefits in the form of royalty payments. For example, in Indianapolis, Indiana, in 2009, the Director of Athletics at North Central High School "noticed shoddy-looking unlicensed merchandise displaying the Panther logo being sold at well-known national retail stores in his area" (Popke 2009, p.1). Generally, there is nothing illegal about the production of merchandise bearing mascots and logos and eventual sale at retail chains. However, once a *legitimate license* is obtained, only then can the schools themselves benefit and have the opportunity to make some revenue through royalty payments.

While college athletic programs have made significant amounts of money through licensed merchandise programs, there wasn't an initiative to provide a licensing program at the interscholastic level until 2009. Consequently, "no attempt had been made to rein in licensees for the entire high school market – which, at 19,000 schools strong, is considered to have the greatest potential for growth among all categories in the licensing universe" (Popke 2009, p.1). As previously mentioned, in 2009 a partnership between the National Federation of State High School Associations (NFHS) and the Licensing Resource Group, LLC (LRG) was formed, their aim being to help and protect schools by controlling unauthorized sales at the large national retail chains. Thus, having a licensed merchandise program is *good business* in terms of the licensor/licensee relationship so that the image and reputation of the school/institution are protected through *quality control* measures and consumers can avoid deception.

In terms of *promotion*, licensed merchandise programs are used as a vehicle to highlight both internal and external support of the school/institution. Additionally, there are many other forms in which licensing can be utilized as a promotional tool. Three promotional objectives of licensing that are generally associated with college athletic programs are the following:

- judicious selection of product category
- brand-oriented analysis
- developing new markets.

In sports fundraising among many college athletic programs, the work and activities of the promotional objectives listed above may be within the organizational function of the Office of Trademarks and Licensing or perhaps the Sports Marketing Department. Regardless of the organizational orientation, this is clearly a revenue stream that colleges and universities have capitalized upon and is a dynamic that has tremendous potential. There are numerous examples of good collegiate licensing programs which utilize licensing as an advertising mechanism to advance the name and/or reputation of the school/institution. The concept of promoting the school and keeping their good name in the *public eye* has three important characteristics; first, the judicious selection of products. Revoyr states "the selection of product to be licensed is the most important process" (1995, p.5). Product selection should be in accord to the educational mission and ethical values of the institution. For example, if alcohol consumption is a *hot-button* issue or a challenge on a particular campus and the administration is working hard at dealing with those issues, it may be *highly inappropriate* to license the school mascot and/or logo on beer products or containers such as shot glasses, pub mugs or other ancillary products. Controlling *how* the logo or mascot is promoted on specific product categories is a key aspect when considering licensing as a promotional tool.

Second, brand-oriented analyses by the athletic program are also an important consideration for those interested in promoting their institutions. For example, in regard to clothing and apparel, product *quality* is a key factor. Schools should be aware of and ultimately have control over the difference between placing a school logo on an unknown brand of clothing, and placing the logo on *Under Armour* or perhaps *Champion* branded clothing and apparel. Having a well-recognized licensee, such as *Under Armour* or *Champion*, conveys credibility in advancing the good name and reputation of the school. In the end, no one wants to see their school have their intellectual property mass-produced by unknown licensees and distributed through *cut-rate* and inferior merchants.

The third characteristic of promotional objectives is through the development of new markets. For example, while schools and their athletic teams are primarily identified by their logos and trademarks, as was previously mentioned, they can also be identified by their school *color schemes*. For example, from a legal perspective, The Ohio State University and their scarlet and gray color scheme has *secondary meaning*, because it is an identifying feature that has been licensed. In 2006, the scarlet and gray colors were "The Home Depot's No. 1-selling collegiate paint scheme in its Team Colors program" (SportsBusiness Daily 2006, p.1). Taken a step further, cultivating a more *youthful* or perhaps a more *female-oriented* consumer could be the target of promotions. *Pink-colored* uniforms, t-shirts, hats, etc. have been produced with the team logos/mascots targeting females, for example. Many schools have also either modified or even created a new and improved looking mascot so that they can be produce teddy bear-like products aimed at the youth market.

Innovative product categories specific to females or the youth market have been successful in many instances. For example, KE Specialties LLC out of New Albany, Ohio introduced unique products with the Ohio State University logo, as well as *Brutus the Buckeye* mascot. Currently, some of the products aimed at the female market that are licensed include Ohio State Buckeye hand sanitizer bottles, fifteen-ounce tubes of lip balm, and team-colored nail polish, just to name a few. For the youth market, they have developed the Ohio State *team growth chart* and team mascot *math flashcards*. Overall, the potential and possibilities are endless, however, the key component to keep in mind when dealing with licensees is the need to control the type of products as well as the brands that are marketed to the new groups that are being cultivated.

The profit-making ability of a well-coordinated licensed merchandising program cannot be underestimated. By licensing a logo, a mascot or a trademark, an athletic department can make a profit from their image without having to invest in the equipment and industry needed to produce and distribute all the clothing and other novelties itself. Clearly, the size and scope of the athletic program will be an influential factor in the profit-making ability of a licensed merchandising program. However, regardless of institutional size, licensing is producing significant new income, does not require a substantial amount of resources (either financial or human) and the profit that is made is mainly *net income*. Revoyr sums up the profitability of licensing by stating, "Licensing income is relatively easy to obtain, does not require large staffs with specialized or expensive training, and it is clean (non-polluting)". In terms of profit potential, "For a mature program that earns $200,000 in licensing income, no more than twenty-five percent of the royalty income should go to expenses (if it does, management should look into the operation or change the operator)" (1995, p.6).

In the end, while some in the intercollegiate athletic domain may proclaim that protection and promotion are primary objectives of their licensing programs, in reality, most are interested in and value making profits.

ROYALTY CALCULATION AND MANAGEMENT

Having access to or hiring legal counsel is a key component when it comes to licensing a mascot, logo, trademark or other type of intellectual property in regard to composing a contracted agreement document. However, when it comes to issues related to the calculation of royalty, sales reporting, payment schedules and other provisions related to record-keeping of intellectual property, this should be prepared with the guidance and expertise of *certified accountants* and *licensing administrators*. Licensing administrators are the *gatekeepers* of the intellectual property within their specific institutions. They protect the institution's name, identifying marks, logos, and reputation by ensuring that all products bearing its name or likeness are of the finest quality and reflect positively on the institution as a whole. Having access to the services of a certified accountant is also important in regard to royalty calculation. Their primary function is to compute periodic royalty revenues and expenses, to ensure that ledger balances are accurate, complete and conform to accepted accounting principles, or GAAP. Overall, "These sections require business experience, not necessarily legal expertise" (Revoyr 1995, p.95). Since licensing administrators are the gatekeepers of intellectual property, licensees pay a royalty on products that are sold. Royalty is the amount charged to the licensee for the continued utilization of the intellectual property and is based on the *wholesale price* of the product. Even though there is not a consistent policy which all universities follow regarding licensing and other facets of intellectual property, many similarities are widespread in university licensing practice, at least in the United States.

In general, there are procedures that the licensing administrator ordinarily manages that can include, but are not limited to the following areas:

- annual minimum royalty guarantees
- up-front licensing fees
- royalty reporting procedures (monthly or quarterly reports).

Annual Minimum Royalty Guarantees

This is an element of the contracted agreement between the licensor and the licensee. It is typically defined in the contract as a *non-refundable/non-transferable annual fee* of a negotiated monetary amount within the contracted year in which the royalties are earned. Overall, the contracted agreement should clearly identify and explain what the minimum guarantees are and whether they are to be paid in the first year of the agreement or in succeeding years. This is an important aspect in developing the agreement due to the fact that "Lacking in many contracts is the provision that if the minimums are not paid after the first year, the licensor has the right to terminate the agreement. It is a good provision to have" (Revoyr 1995, p.97). Moreover, depending upon the *product category*, annual minimum royalty guarantees can vary.

For example, a licensor may negotiate that in the category of *T-shirts* the licensee pays a $200 annual fee. Consequently, licensors may charge a lower annual royalty guarantee in the category of *key-chain holders* or *logoed-bumper stickers*. Fundamentally, the primary role of these annual minimum royalty guarantees is to incentivize licensees to perform, to produce, distribute and/or sell plenty of licensed merchandise within their product category to cover the annual minimum. In other words, the annual fee is essentially a *diligence* provision for performance.

Otherwise, "In fact, lack of performance (e.g. failure to achieve royalty minimums) has been found to be one of the most prevalent criteria for nonrenewal or revocation of agreements" (Irwin, Sutton and McCarthy 2002, p.259).

Up-front Licensing Fees

The up-front license issue fee is a one-time fee due at the execution of the license agreement, or on an otherwise negotiated/agreed-upon payment schedule. In some cases, these fees are bundled along with the annual minimum royalty guarantee. The amount of this fee is related to the value of the rights granted to the licensee, whether or not the licensee has *exclusive or non-exclusive rights. Exclusive licenses,* which are generally more expensive, grant a licensee sole rights to intellectual property, typically within a defined or limited field of use. Another license can be granted for the intellectual property, but not within the same field. *Non-exclusive licenses* grant multiple licensees rights to intellectual property within a defined *field of use.* Typically, "field of use" defines the parameters of the business world that the intellectual property can be used in.

At the intercollegiate level, the CLC or the *Collegiate Licensing Company,* out of Atlanta, Georgia, is a significant third-party licensing intermediary that represents numerous colleges, universities, athletic conferences, and championship bowl games among other institutions. In fact, the CLC is owned by IMG Worldwide, previously known as International Management Group, a global sports, fashion and media business.

In 2005, the University of Texas, a client of the CLC, led the nation in licensing revenue at $8.2 million in royalties. Accordingly, "T-shirts were the top-sellers for UT, followed by hats. After the Longhorns beat USC in the Rose Bowl, the school's 450 licensees sold everything from key chains to mini football helmets to a Waterford crystal football. Even coach Mack Brown's photo on the Wheaties cereal box brought in money" (The Associated Press 2006, p.1). At the time, Texas had a standard royalty rate of eight percent compared to the twelve percent royalty rate they had on national championship merchandise items (The Associated Press 2006, p.1).

Overall, the major point to be understood is that granting either exclusive or non-exclusive licenses is generally within the domain of *how* the agreement is drafted and negotiated by the licensor's and licensee's legal counsel. Thus, the process of licensing can be cumbersome and as such, the *contemporary trend* has been for universities to outsource the licensing operations to the services of a third-party licensing intermediary.

Royalty Reporting Procedures (monthly or quarterly reports)

The royalty reporting procedures are another important feature of the licensing agreement. One of the most significant aspects of this type of reporting is, in general, through the negotiated *frequency* of how the financial information is submitted from the licensee to the licensor. In some cases, royalty reports are submitted on a quarterly basis, others on a monthly basis. Typically, large companies with multiple licenses report royalty on a monthly basis. Consequently, as Revoyr states, "Smaller companies with few licenses may have to remain on the quarterly schedule, which is the minimum allowable" (1995, p.99). Beyond the frequency of the reports, another important facet regarding the reporting procedures is the amount of *detail* that is contained within the reports themselves. If there is specific information that your department is interested in, then that must be clearly communicated with the licensee. Some licensees may send a very simplified report that states the total sales for the month or quarter and the amount of royalty money owed. Ideally, reports should contain much more information than just the basic sales information and royalty owed.

For example, "the report should break down each product by style and numbers sold, how many T-shirts, how many sweatshirts, how many shorts, etc., giving both the numbers sold and the total sales price" (Revoyr 1995, p.99). By getting the details on specific merchandise categories and by *tracking* that type of information from month to month or from quarter to quarter, this will ultimately shed some light in understanding and determining which products sell well or those that don't. "Watching such details will give the program manager insights into trends as to which products are gaining or losing in popularity, and which retail markets are doing the same. Such trends will also point out whether the brand is gaining or losing in popularity" (Revoyr 1995, p.100). In the end, it is up to the licensor to ensure that the reports and the associated royalty checks are accurate and as such, there should be language in the agreements they have with licensees that gives the licensor the right to review the licensee's books.

Some nationally recognized youth sport organizations, such as Little League Baseball and Softball as well as Pop Warner Football, already have licensing programs in place. Furthermore, Pop Warner has a *vendor program* which is intended to authorize local Pop Warner programs to do business with local vendors in their communities, while promoting the Pop Warner brand.

As was detailed previously, the process of licensing can become cumbersome, depending upon the amount of detailed information the licensor requires of each licensee. While it is certainly possible to manage all aspects of a licensing program *in-house* through the trademark department, a large licensing agency acting as an intermediary between the sport organization and the licensee can offer many advantages. Thus, the *contemporary trend* has been for universities to outsource the licensing operations to the services of a third-party licensing intermediary. Companies like the CLC or even the partnership previously detailed between the National Federation of State High School Associations (NFHS) and the Licensing Resource Group, LLC (LRG), mean that clients can benefit from the experience and resources a licensing firm can bring to the table, especially when negotiating agreements with multiple licensees.

HOW MAXIMIZING POINTS OF SALE INFLUENCES FUNDRAISING

Among school-based athletic programs, it has been illustrated that the primary sources of revenue are among *ticket sales, concessions and licensed merchandise sales*. The goal of this chapter was to provide a comprehensive understanding of how maximizing all potential points of sale is significant in influencing *fundraising*. While these three points of sale may not be considered as "fundraising" to some, the fundamental concept to keep in mind is to understand *why* the combination of creating new revenue streams via fundraisers and capitalizing upon the existing points of sale (tickets, concessions and licensed merchandise) is substantially relevant in administering an athletic/sports organization.

Fundraising in sport does not exist in a vacuum and is interdependent on sale of tickets, concessions and licensed merchandise. Practically speaking, if your sport organization has poor attendance at events, it logically follows that if the three areas are neglected, eventually *expenses will outpace revenues*. Therefore, how does one ask the public or stakeholders to invest/donate to an organization that doesn't even consider the importance of driving up attendance through these profit-oriented elements? What would motivate a donor or a corporate sponsor to invest their money into a sport organization that does not capitalize on various ticketing strategies to drive attendance, and is content with selling warm beer, cold food and cheaply produced logo garments? Several studies have examined the empirical relationship between attendance at athletic events and charitable contributions to institutions of higher education and will be listed at the end of the chapter.

In conclusion, among the interscholastic athletic domain in the United States, athletic directors are faced with pressures of limiting or eliminating team travel to long-distance contest destinations, reducing the number of games/contests, or in many instances, figuring out whether specific teams and/or programs continue to survive or are eliminated. Youth-oriented sport organizations in the United States, such as Little League Baseball are dependent on *ancillary points of sale*. Besides registration fees, the primary source of revenue for many youth baseball programs is among concession stands and parents volunteering their time and effort to raise those funds. This is therefore vital to the ongoing financial health of the youth league. There is an interesting and *dynamic relationship* between the aforementioned points of sale and fundraising, and it merits further research and investigation.

FURTHER READING

Bouchet, A., Ballouli, K. and Bennett, G. (2011) "Implementing a Ticket Sales Force in College Athletics: A Decade of Challenges", *Sport Marketing Quarterly*, 20 (2) 84–92, available at search.epnet.com.

Carroll, M. S. (2009) "Development of a scale to measure perceived risk in collegiate spectator sport and assess its impact on sport consumption intentions", University of Florida, available at http://search.proquest.com/docview/304882365?accountid=2909 (accessed 01/31/12).

Cozart, E. S. (2010) "The relationship between the online secondary ticket market and college athletics", University of North Carolina at Chapel Hill, available at http://search.proquest.com/docview/821547171?accountid=2909 (accessed 01/31/12).

Cunningham, G. B. and Kwon, H. (2003) "The theory of planned behavior and intentions to attend a sport event", *Sport Management Review*, 6, 127–145.

Greenwell, T. C. (2007) "Expectations, industry standards, and customer satisfaction in the student ticket process", *Sport Marketing Quarterly*, 16, 7–14.

Halley, J. (2010) "High schools cash in on logos, avoid clashes with colleges", *USA Today*, available at http://www.usatoday.com/sports/preps/2010-12-06-high-school-logos-trademark_N.htm (accessed 01/31/12).

Irwin, R., Sutton, W. and McCarthy, L. (2002) *Sports promotion and sales management*, Champaign, Illinois: Human Kinetics.

Kwon, H. H. and Armstrong, K. L. (2006) "Impulse purchases of sport team licensed merchandise: What matters?" *Journal of Sport Management*, 20, 101–119.

Laverie, D. L. and Arnett, D. B. (2000) "Factors affecting fan attendance: The influence of identity salience and satisfaction", *Journal of Leisure Research*, 32, 225–246.

Matsuoka, H., Chelladurai, P. and Harada, M. (2003) "Direct and interaction effects of team identification and satisfaction on intention to attend games", *Sport Marketing Quarterly*, 12, 244–253.

Popke, Michael (2009) "Merch madness: A new nationwide licensing program could help high schools generate new revenue and protect their image", available at http://athleticbusiness.com/articles/article.aspx?articleid=2601&zoneid=34 (accessed 01/31/12).

Shank, M. D. (2004) *Sports marketing: a strategic perspective* (3rd edn), Saddle River, NJ: Prentice Hall.

Steinbach, P. (2008) "Concessions – Concessions contracts capitalizing on consumers' brand loyalty", available at http://athleticbusiness.com/articles/article.aspx?articleid=1838&zoneid=37 (accessed 01/31/12).

Trail, G. T., Anderson, D. F. and Fink, J. S. (2000) "A theoretical model of sport spectator consumption behavior", *International Journal of Sport Management*, 1, 154–180.

—— (2005) "Consumer satisfaction and identity theory: A model of sport spectator conative loyalty", *Sport Marketing Quarterly*, 14 (2) 98–111.

APPLICATION/SKILL BUILDING EXERCISE

Exercise 1: for students

Select a college/university, a youth sport organization or a high school of your choice to examine/study. Make an effort to contact the Youth Sport Administrator or Program Director or the Director of Athletics at that particular school and college/university. Set up a face-to-face interview or perhaps a phone interview based on the administrator's availability/schedule. Based on the chapter lesson regarding "points of sale" and profit-making relative to *ticket sales*, *concession sales* and *licensed merchandise sales*, engage the administrator to answer the following questions among the following areas:

- Among the three primary revenue producing areas (ticket sales, concession sales and licensed merchandise sales); what do they perceive as:
  - A The most significant revenue producer?
  - B The area that has the greatest potential for development/growth?
- Based on the administrator's perception, to what extent do *social media/social networking sites* such as Facebook and/or Twitter impact upon the marketing of tickets to generate more revenue for their athletic program?
- From the administrator's experience dealing with season ticket holders or stakeholders in general:
  - A What strategies do they use to *incentivize* fans/spectators to attend athletic events?
  - B To what extent do they solicit *feedback* from their season ticket holders or stakeholders and what methodologies do they

employ? (i.e. suggestion boxes, e-mail, survey instruments, booster meetings, focus groups)?

- According to the administrator, what is the current status of their concessions operations; is it an *in-house* operation or is it outsourced to a *third-party* intermediary such as an Aramark, Sodexo or Delaware North Company?

- In terms of a "licensing program", according to the administrator:
  - A Is the program operation *in-house* or is it outsourced to a *third-party intermediary* such as the Collegiate Licensing Company (CLC) or the Licensing Resource Group, LLC (LRG)?
  - B What is the approximate "royalty rate percentage" they charge licensees?
  - C (If a youth or interscholastic athletic director) Do they sell licensed merchandise in the community at retail stores and if so, does the school or youth sport organizations make a profit from those sales? If not or unknown to them, is the Athletic Director *aware* of the partnership between the National Federation of State High School Associations (NFHS) and the Licensing Resource Group, LLC (LRG)?

Exercise 2: for practitioners

Based on the chapter lesson regarding "points of sale" and profit-making relative to *ticket sales*, *concession sales* and *licensed merchandise sales*, make a candid effort to answer the following questions among the following areas:

- Among the three primary revenue producing areas (ticket sales, concession sales and licensed merchandise sales); what do they perceive as:
  - A The most significant revenue producer?
  - B The area that has the greatest potential for development/growth?

- To what extent do *social media/social networking* sites such as Facebook and/or Twitter impact upon the marketing of tickets to generate more revenue for your athletic program?

- In dealing with season ticket holders or stakeholders in general:
  - A What strategies do you use to *incentivize* fans/spectators to attend athletic events?
  - B What kind of *feedback* do you receive from your season ticket holders or stakeholders and what methodologies do you employ to obtain it (i.e. suggestion boxes, e-mail, survey instruments, booster meetings, focus groups)?
  - C Based on your answer in subsection B, can you identify potential areas to improve communications with your season ticket holders/stakeholders?

- What is the current status of your concessions operations; is it an *in-house operation* or is it outsourced to a *third-party intermediary* such as an Aramark, Sodexo or Delaware North Company?

- Based on the current status of your concession operations, identify and explain the top five advantages and top five disadvantages. Can you determine if outsourcing your concession operations to a third party is worthwhile?

- In terms of a licensed merchandise program at your institution:
  - A Is the program operation *in-house* or is it outsourced to a *third-party intermediary* such as the Collegiate Licensing Company (CLC) or the Licensing Resource Group, LLC (LRG)?
  - B What is the approximate "royalty rate percentage" you charge licensees?
  - C Based on your answer to sub-section B, can you determine if outsourcing your logos, marks, and other intellectual property to a licensing company such as CLC or LRG is worthwhile?
  - D (If a youth or interscholastic athletic director) Does your school or youth sport organization have a licensed merchandise program? If so, does your school or youth sport organizations actually make a profit from those sales? If not or if unknown, are you *aware* of the partnership between the National Federation of State High School Associations (NFHS) and the Licensing Resource Group, LLC (LRG)?

CHAPTER 8

WORKING WITH DIVERSE CONSTITUENCIES: CULTIVATION STRATEGIES AND ESSENTIAL RESOURCES

The purpose of this chapter is to analyze and focus attention on the organizational aspects and the associated resources needed to work successfully with diverse constituencies and/or stakeholders of the athletic program. The concepts, strategies and systems to successfully manage these groups of people include, but are not limited to, the following:

- organizational considerations and requisite resources
- cultivation strategies and prospect management systems
- the donor focused orientation.

In terms of organization, it is necessary to understand and appreciate the *fundraising environment* that exists among the majority of athletic programs in the United States. On page 136, is a basic illustration of the environment that supports the athletic organization. Dr William Stier developed a model to represent this concept (see Figure 8.1). However, a fundamental consideration that is *foundational* to fund-raising success that needs to be developed well before reaching out to the fundraising environment is the *virtuousness* of the sports organization itself. Therefore, as was detailed in Chapter 1 as a prerequisite, creating and/or developing a well-defined mission statement of your sport organization as well as building a positive image that is based on ethical principles is a key element in the dynamic, multifaceted nature of sports fundraising. Building from this foundational consideration, those key individuals within the sport organization who administer the programs are responsible for creating awareness with an ethical approach to projecting the organization's image to the public at large,

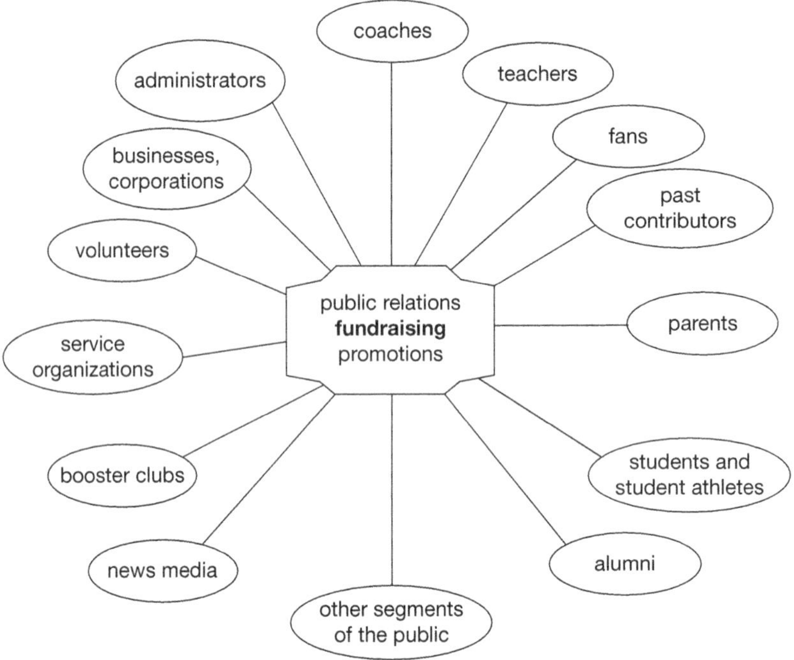

Figure 8.1 Identification of Role Players in the Support of Sports

Source: Stier Jr., W. F. (2001) *Fundraising for Sport*, Boston, MA: American Press, p.32.

as well as their target constituencies. In general, careful and judicious development of the aforementioned *awareness* and *image projection* is central to fundraising success among the fundraising environment.

As Stier states, "Without it, one's effectiveness is questionable, if not nonexistent" (2001, p.32). Overall, the time and effort it takes to implement all of the fundraising strategies and tactics, with the aim of obtaining as much internal and external financial support as possible, can be significantly diminished without having the ability of advancing an ethical and straightforward image of the sport organization.

ORGANIZING CONSTITUENCIES AND REQUISITE RESOURCES

Building upon the foundation of having a straightforward and virtuous sport organization to promote to the fundraising environment, is the process of identifying, organizing and managing the proper collection, selection and development of information about your stakeholders/constituency and synthesizing that into meaningful data.

Overall, there are a variety of ways in which stakeholders and/or constituencies are identified and subsequently managed and organized at the intercollegiate athletic level. Furthermore, there is an opportunity for youth and high school athletic programs to learn lessons from the intercollegiate athletic domain. These include, but are not limited to the following:

- fundraising diversification (short- and long-term strategies)
- stakeholder identification
- organization of stakeholders
- requisite resources
- data collection plans.

Fundraising among a variety of sport organizations is mainly carried out by practices that are *quick-fix* in their strategic orientation. This chapter is aimed at providing an appreciation and understanding of the unique constellation of dynamics and processes that ultimately demonstrate the benefits of creating a more *donor focused approach* that will, in the end, lead to stronger relationships for the long term that are mutually beneficial for both the donor and the sport organization. Thus, an important aspect that needs to be addressed is the concept of fundraising diversification.

Fundraising Diversification

Fundraising diversification is an important concept for both youth and high school athletic organizations to acknowledge if they want to have success in both the short and long term. The organizational goal is to have the *requisite resources* to manage multiple streams of income and to strike a balance among them. For the better part of the last three decades among youth and many high school athletic programs, fundraising has been conducted as a short-term activity to satisfy specific needs of the program, from new uniforms for the football players, to new bats for the baseball team to updated equipment for the girls' soccer team. While the specific needs may change over the years, the methods of obtaining the funds have, for the most part, remained the same. *Episodic fundraisers* are activities where the sport organization sells products and/or services to generate funds for a specific short-term goal. These approaches are traditionally the way in which the majority of youth sport organizations and many high school athletic departments raise funds for their programs. This will be covered in more detail later in this chapter. However, the main idea to keep in mind is that although episodic fundraisers are a reality, they should not be the only method in which fundraisers are conducted.

In addition to episodic funding events, there need to be *long-term strategies* and *data collection plans*. The forthcoming material presented in this chapter will cover cultivation strategies such as relationship management as well as the basics of prospect management and associated systems. Overall, the key contribution here is to provide a basic overview of the elements that can be applicable to a variety of sport organizations.

There have been numerous research studies conducted in this area referred to as *donor development* or *prospect management*, and how these relationship marketing theories can be applied across a variety of environments. There will be an assortment of research studies and other resources acknowledged and cited at the end of this chapter for further investigation. The intent of this chapter lies in the presentation of *applied* fundraising strategies and systems that go beyond the shotgun approaches that many sport organizations implement.

Stakeholder Identification

As a college or high school-based athletic department, or perhaps even a youth-oriented sport organization for that matter, you seldom control who your stakeholders happen to be. However, the good news is "you have tremendous control over how you spend your time and resources" (Birkholtz 2008, p.73), in order to boost your relationship with them. Consequently, among intercollegiate athletic programs, you should have an athletic development officer who fully comprehends the mission of the athletic organization as well as its case to garner financial support. The more understandably these elements are shared with stakeholders and prospective donors, the quicker you can move toward the *solicitation phase* of the fundraising cycle. As a cautionary element, a gift can be asked for too early in the process based on the individual donors' relationship with the sport organization. Thus, all prospective donors as well as secured donors are unique and as such, the approaches and/or strategies one employs to successfully solicit must be sensitive to their values, needs and aspirations.

Organization of Stakeholders

As was mentioned previously, both prospective and secured donors need to be solicited in such a way that is sensitive to their values, needs and aspirations. Taken a step further, the best practice in fundraising in terms of organizing these diverse stakeholders is a concerted *team approach* as opposed to a single entity or fragmented group approach. By incorporating a team approach, you are able to unite multiple skills and competencies. A group of key stakeholders of the athletic program can reach more individuals, businesses, alumni groups, parents, and teachers, for example, compared to a single individual. Furthermore, within that group, a *core team of committed stakeholders* can generate more money in a quicker and more efficient fashion than one person, regardless of how great that person may be at raising funds. Therefore, combining the human resources to form a teamed structure has the capacity for more realistic success than a single person or the fragmented efforts of single activity booster groups. For example, to have the baseball boosters, the track and field boosters and the band boosters all blitzing the community simultaneously in episodic fundraisers, puts substantial stress on community members to buy products and or services without proper warning or notification. Therefore, if the needs of specific sports teams/groups are carried out in a well-planned and organized fundraiser that teams up the needs of activities such as baseball, track and field as well as the band, more success can occur, as opposed to having these teams/groups solicit funds in a scattered, unorganized manner.

Paradoxically, many sport organizations implement a *shotgun approach*, whereby they send their athletes, parents, volunteers and anyone else they can find to go out into the community and sell products and/or services to generate funds for a specific short-term goal. These short-term episodic fundraisers can include any type of product and/or service ranging from selling candy bars, gift-wrap, scented candles or even pre-paid debit cards.

Furthermore, actually selling these products is quite challenging, even for the most trained sales professionals who do this on a full-time basis. As a result, it is practically impossible for student athletes and usually results in fundraising frustration and failure. Moreover, the companies who promote and profit from having their candy bars or pre-paid debit cards sold usually have fifty percent of the money raised go back to them. So, if your athletic organization is able to raise $2,000 in selling candy bars, in most cases, $1,000 will go back to the company. Without going into too much detail on this type of fundraising approach, having your athletes sell products and services for companies that end up taking half of the overall sales is an unreasonable expectation and a waste of time and effort. Therefore, the type of episodic fundraiser and the actual percentage of profit that goes back to the sport organization must be carefully contemplated.

Organization is a key function that often does not get the attention it deserves, and this can lead to fundraising frustration among all groups involved. This is especially apparent at the youth sport level where the majority of the sport programs are administered on inadequate budgets and simultaneously staffed by untrained parent volunteers. As highlighted in Chapter 1, there are a multitude of books and dissertation studies, as well as countless articles published over the last two decades that highlight the problematic aspects of youth sports. These include, but are not limited to, the following five areas:

- participation/dropout rates
- supervision and competency issues among volunteer coaches
- psychological/burnout issues among youth sport participants
- physiological issues from over-training
- over-emphasis on competition over instruction.

While these issues are significant and meritorious, research regarding the costs associated with those who participate on nationally-sponsored youth sports, elite-level club sports or recreational sport programs and the need for *fundraising* is lacking in comparison to the five areas listed above. Furthermore, the status of youth sports as *lacking administrative leadership* has been well-documented, as well as the fact that they are heavily dependent upon parents and volunteers.

Consequently, fundraising initiatives reflect the unorganized and incompetent leadership in many cases. Along with the financial challenges of a sluggish economy or perhaps increased competition from other charitable organizations, and the issues referenced earlier among youth sport, the prospect of leading one of these programs can be daunting. This is where the education and training of the next generation of sport administration leaders is vitally important for *administrative reform*, as covered in Chapter 3. This call for reform needs to take place in our schools of higher education among the sport administration/sport management programs. Otherwise, the vicious cycle of insufficient and in many cases inappropriate fundraising activities will continue to plague youth sports as well as high school athletics in America.

Requisite Resources

In terms of the lack of a *long-term orientation* and the *organizational and administrative issues* involving coordinating stakeholders, there are distinguishable differences between the fundraising activities conducted at the college level compared to high school and youth sport organizations.

Other distinguishable differences among all three categories pertain to human and financial resources, and a clear grasp of the *fundraising taxonomy*; in other words, where each level fits on the proverbial *totem pole*. Nevertheless, despite these differences when it comes to raising funds, there are fundamental principles, techniques, models, guidelines and challenges to effectively plan, communicate, implement and manage that are applicable among all levels. These differences generally include, but are not limited to, the following:

- the division of athletic departments
- the school size (enrollment)
- the number of sports offered

- the number of athletes
- the ratio of male to female athletes.

Therefore, every college, high school or youth sport organization is *situationally specific*. In terms of empirical data-driven research, it is surprising to note that studies specific to athletic fundraising and/or budgeting are lacking existence. It is common knowledge among the athletic administration profession that the larger the athletic departments are within Division I athletics, the larger their budget and the more fundraising resources they have. However, the empirical inquiry, in order to glean further insight about this phenomenon, is meager. Therefore, new research into the similarities and differences of the fundraising activities among and between athletic departments/sport organizations is warranted.

The necessary or *requisite* resources to plan, implement and evaluate a successful fundraising initiative for a sport organization are quite diverse and there is no one singular answer. Unfortunately, this is the aspect of fundraising that often does not receive the attention it requires. However, there is a five-step process that, if approached pragmatically, can yield desirable results. Regardless of orientation and size of the resources, fundraising for the most part, includes, but is not limited to, the following:

- identifying your internal and external stakeholders
- determining the essential needs of your stakeholders and ensuring that those exact needs are taken care of robustly
- assuring that the fundraising event and/or activities don't conflict with the collective orientation of the community
- activating those individuals who have the skills, energies, talents, abilities and knowledge to raise money into a unified team
- evaluating the results in a timely manner.

As was detailed in earlier chapters, steps one and two are fundamental *prerequisites* to the process. Success in fundraising is a *trial and error* endeavor, but overall, it is vitally important not to overlook step three. The events and activities that are planned and coordinated should not conflict with the prevailing tenor and/or collective orientation of the community. Having a true understanding of the *culture* of the community toward fundraising is a dynamic that cannot be overestimated. Step four has been well documented in Chapter 6. *Teaming* and simultaneously motivating those individuals and/or stakeholders who have the skills, energies, talents, abilities and knowledge to raise money is much more efficient and effective than the alternative. One of the most overlooked aspects of the process is *evaluating the results* and the subsequent collection of pertinent data to retain for future reference.

Having the ability to determine what worked or didn't work, or perhaps what needed improvement or modification, is the *aim* of evaluating the results. Were the pre-determined fundraising goals achieved or not? This question cannot be appropriately answered or judged without a proper assessment and this should be done while the information is relatively fresh in the minds of those involved. Therefore, the need to identify and reveal the successful activities so that they can be preserved and replicated is important to record. Simultaneously modifying or improving the other fundraising activities that were not so financially successful will lead to more fundraising success in the future.

Thus, evaluating the results and keeping refined records and/or documentation allows the sport organization to build on previous success and avoid past failures.

Data Collection Plans

How does one effectively and efficiently collect, store and manage informational and numeric data to aid in guiding fundraising decisions? Chapter 4 affirmed and illustrated the various ways in which both *hard data* and *soft data* elements can be categorized and eventually converted into meaningful *numeric data*. Overall, the primary objective of the entire process of data collection is to be able to glean meaningful information, and present it in a reliable format. If that primary objective is accomplished, this statistical tool will allow your athletic organization to make good, accurate and efficient decisions about your donors, prospective donors and other fundraising initiatives. As was detailed at the outset of this chapter, this is exactly where the fundamental differences lie among college athletic programs compared to high school and youth sport organizations.

However, this is precisely the point where both high school and youth sport organizations have an opportunity to expand their horizons beyond the annual episodic fundraiser. The following information presented in this chapter will aid in facilitating fundraising efforts through the concepts of cultivation strategies and prospect management systems in addition to a *donor focused orientation*. Overall, there is significant *value* in the forthcoming prospect management systems and donor focused strategies, regardless of the size, position, and/or financial status of the sport organization.

CULTIVATION STRATEGIES AND PROSPECT MANAGEMENT SYSTEMS

When taking a closer analysis of the concept of *cultivation*, it is evident that it is a multifaceted process. Defining what that process entails is challenging, yet necessary to appropriately address and reach diverse constituencies and/or stakeholders of the athletic program. Therefore, without too much complexity, cultivation is a process that takes into consideration the building of relationships among prospects and donors (Carlson 2000). In a nutshell, the process of cultivation is when you combine all of the planning activities as well as the various modes of communication to arouse people to make a financial donation to your sport organization. Cultivation is a very *personal endeavor*; individuals want to be treated as individuals, not like a number. Moreover, as well as having the requisite resources that were previously detailed, when it comes to cultivation, a *team approach* is the best practice. Carlson (2000) succinctly explains this by indicating that one person alone cannot do it all by themselves. They need the assistance of a team, as there are not enough hours in the workday to establish a personal relationship with every prospective and current donor.

Taken a step further, relative to the varied modes of communication to help arouse people to donate money to your sport organization is the consideration of both *conventional* and *unconventional* ways in which to communicate with the stakeholders of your sport program. For example, we are constantly having discussions with our stakeholders, whether they take place on the phone, in the gymnasium, via e-mails and/or text messages, or perhaps even in the newspaper or at tailgate hospitality tents outside of the football stadium. It goes on perpetually whether we realize it or not. From the formal fundraising letters, alumni newsletters and annual drive phone solicitations, to informal modes such as a random encounter at the grocery store, at restaurants or even at the gas station, all of these forms of communication create impressions among stakeholders and form perceptions about your sport organization, whether they are positive or negative. The fundamental element here is to understand and appreciate the importance of having a clear mission statement and transmitting a positive image. Specific components that lead to successful cultivation can include, but are not limited to the following four questions, which your sport organization should consider:

- What is the public's perception of our sport organization?
- Are who and what our sport organization really happens to be clearly and accurately perceived by the public?
- Do all of the various modes of communication that originate from our sport organization accurately reflect our mission and values?
- If not, how can we improve our cultivation techniques so we can ultimately present a better image that we truly want to communicate to the public?

Thus, fundraising success lies within the ability to have all conventional and unconventional communications about the sport organization clearly reflect and foster its mission and image. While this is a challenging undertaking, those sport organizations that pay particular attention to getting people involved through hands-on cultivation activities through a team-oriented approach *position* themselves very well, because when they do solicit for financial support, those people are most likely to react by giving generously to the sport organization, based on their involvement. Additionally, the particular dynamics involving the characteristics and realities of the constituency/stakeholders is an aspect of cultivation that's often overlooked. Worth states that "colleges and universities too often strive to replicate programs they observe and admire at very different types of institutions" (2002, p.21). To clearly understand the importance of this point, consider the analogy of a small, rural high school basketball program and a newly hired coach decides to implement the *Duke University* motion offense. While this is a great offensive strategy, one has to consider whether or not the players at this particular rural school have the discipline, ball control and skills to implement it. Overall, you can't change the players but you can change your strategy.

Many high level administrators who make up the *core* of the constituency encourage the implementation of programs and fundraising initiatives that have been successful elsewhere, without necessarily taking the time to consider their suitability in a highly different set of circumstances. All too often, there are rationalizations that *if it works there, it can work here*, and this can be a misguided risk. As a result, "Allocation of staff and budget among the various elements of the program should reflect a careful analysis of the institution's academic programs, needs, and history, as well as the capacities and inclinations of its constituency" (Worth 2002, p.22). If fundraising success is to be realized, careful assessment of the constituency and/or stakeholders of the athletic organization must be a priority and in the end, the cultivation strategies utilized should reflect the environmental/economic conditions in which the athletic organization exists.

In the end analysis, cultivation plays a significant role and the strategies should employ an agenda for engaging both donors and potential donors. Moreover, "The key isn't so much the technique, but rather the spirit behind the technique that is important" (Hodge 2003, p.92). The concept of cultivation isn't so much about *your sport organization* as it is really about those you serve and those who give their time and money to ensure the sport organization prospers. Thus, emphasis is on *donor relationship development* rather than just fundraising; contributions should be viewed as investments and a return on investment in this sense is a *return on values* and what they care about.

Prospect Management Systems

The concept of prospect management is a multifaceted proposition. However, in a simplified nutshell, prospect management basically involves taking specific information about potential donors and systematically collecting and recording that information and converting it into meaningful data. The multifaceted aspect to it involves the type and amount of information/data to be collected and recorded, as well as how that information/data is stored and utilized. Consequently, "All of the information in the world will not help raise money unless time is spent analyzing it and applying it to the cultivation process needed to secure repeat gifts, upgraded gifts, special gifts, major gifts and ultimately planned gifts" (Nudd 2003, p.359).

The use of technology, whether it is in the form of a manual spreadsheet system or an integrated database program that manipulates large volumes of data, is no longer just recommended, rather it is a *requirement*. The fundamental objective is to ascertain what components a system *must have* for capturing and examining informational data; this is an essential element if fundraising success is to be realized. Therefore, taking into account the fundamental framework presented in Chapter 4 – planning and goal setting, identifying and targeting the constituency, rallying support and involvement, organizing and managing time, money and resources and evaluating the results – all of this information needs to be systematically organized, collected and recorded into a meaningful data collection system. Regardless of the type of system used for data entry, those staff and/or volunteers who are involved in the collection and entry of this data must be educated on why the system is necessary and how it supports and/or reinforces the fundraising activity. Furthermore, the following options are an important consideration when contemplating the integration of technology:

- the system must be user-friendly
- the people involved in data entry/creating the reports must understand the standardized format
- the process should be evaluated and updated at regular intervals.

One of the pitfalls of adopting new technologies is the challenge of getting people to use it, which is primarily a training issue. However, compatibility can become an issue if the system being utilized is too difficult to apply. Second, the people involved in entering the data must understand the standardized format. In other words, the old idiom "everyone must be on the same page" is imperative. Moreover, there shouldn't be any ambiguity and everyone involved in data entry, whether it's in a manual spreadsheet or a complex database, must all be trained on how to accomplish the task in a standardized format.

Finally, the process should be evaluated and updated at regular intervals. Thus, questions that should be raised and answered at this stage include: are the data entry systems being currently used antiquated or obsolete? Is the system being used actually producing the type of output that was predetermined? How functional or useful are the current computers? How often do the computers need additional maintenance and/or have technical support issues? Is there new software in the marketplace that better meets our needs?

Weaving modern technology into the sport organization doesn't necessarily need to break the budget. There are a significant number of services that are free or are a nominal cost to acquire, especially if your sport organization is not for profit, as is the case for many youth-oriented sport organizations. Simultaneously, there is a substantial range of products and services that involve both hardware and software components. The number of systems and applications can be overwhelming, especially for even the most high-tech sport organization.

Regardless of the type of computerized system that is utilized, there are three basic precepts to understand and appreciate if success in fundraising is to be achieved. First, technology needs to be viewed as a means to an end and not as the end itself. In other words, the process of integrating the diverse information into a standardized and manageable format can consume a considerable amount of time and energy. Therefore, since fundraising is the key activity, it can easily be sidetracked by the integration of a new computerized system and take time away from what is really important. At the same time, the system that is utilized should bring about increased attention to detail, productivity and accountability as opposed to a lack of direction and inefficiency.

Second, it should make communication more efficient and cost-effective as well as save time. For example, as was previously detailed in Chapter 4, if the budget only allows $7,000 for physical postal mailings and it has been five years since the demographic living/deceased category has been updated, utilizing technology to *omit* the deceased individuals from the database can save a significant amount of money. Moreover, technology allows quicker and more efficient utilization of your daily processes. For instance, is the management of one constituent category, such as alumni donors within the database a single category or are they a part of a larger category that includes faculty and employees? Are the systems used integrated? If not, you could be treating the same person as if they were two different people because you might have alumni who are also employees or perhaps alumni who are also faculty members. Therefore, you could potentially be sending out two physical mailings when only one is truly necessary. This is where technology can help manage these potential glitches and curtail wasteful spending.

Finally, the computerized system should also be viewed as a *relationship management tool*. Successful fundraising is concentrated primarily with your capacity to cultivate and oversee relationships with your stakeholders and technology can help track valuable information. For instance, technology has the capacity to aid in managing information efficiently, from the storage capacity of basic demographics of your stakeholders, to tracking the number of phone calls, personalized physical mailings or e-mail alerts that contain announcements for social gatherings. As a result, this kind of system will aid in avoiding the *duplication of effort* by staff and/or volunteers and ultimately increase productivity.

Overall, success in sports fundraising requires much more than technology, but if the technology currently being used does not improve processes or help manage data, then extra work and lost productivity will result in the long term. Technology is a means to an end and should be viewed as such. The goal of technology is to make processes and data management more efficient by providing a system that *seamlessly* facilitates the work of everyone involved.

THE DONOR FOCUSED ORIENTATION AND GENDER DIFFERENCES

As has been thoroughly documented in the previous pages of this book, fundraising is a multifaceted process. Moreover, a growing perception among many youth sport and interscholastic athletic organizations across the United States is to view fundraising apathetically as an *event focused* type of obligation. These sport organizations, in general, do not communicate or market themselves as *mission-driven* organizations that are benefitting the community by helping young people learn and develop skills such as teamwork, social skills, self-confidence, and dealing with success and failure. Often, these highly regarded outcomes of sport participation unfortunately get overlooked when there are other charitable organizations that demonstrate very clearly how they aid starving children in poorer countries, or perhaps display the benefits of supporting cancer research. Therefore, the lack of a clearly tailored mission statement compounded with the over-reliance on episodic type fundraisers that fall short of their goals have caused considerable frustration among many youth and interscholastic sport program administrators and their participants. Simultaneous to the fundraising discouragement, community members have grown cynical as well. One of the key drivers of this cynicism is that donors are more knowledgeable about fraud and embezzlement as a whole. Combined with this cynical attitude has been the proliferation of technology and its implementation. Donors want to be treated as individuals who have attitudes, opinions, feelings and values, and while highly rational and *streamlined*, communication methods such as e-mails, automated telephone systems, and registration/donation landing pages on the Internet tend to taint the human element to fundraising.

In the arena of philanthropy among institutions of higher education, there have been many references in the literature as to the importance of donors' views and motivations. There are many who underscore the importance of analyzing the attitudes and opinions of donors before deciding which methods should be appropriately utilized to solicit them (Williams 1997). Moreover, the gist of a *donor-focused* fund-raising strategy is that success ultimately depends on the degree to which fundraisers treat their donors as individuals with distinctive interests and essential needs, rather than treating them with the typical high volume, callous mass marketing schemes used to promote their cause (Williams 1997). This type of strategy has been successful in the area of higher education philanthropy as well as among specific inter-collegiate athletic programs. Accordingly, an area of opportunity for the youth sport and interscholastic levels is to initiate a donor focused strategy into their fundraising repertoire. As was covered in Chapter 3, contemporary athletic leadership and fundraising is about developing a shared sense of destiny with current and prospective donors.

As donor motivation comes from within the individual, it is the job of the athletic development and/or athletic advancement office to figure out what motivates their cultivated donors and *create* the appropriate environment. Thus, if season tickets, special parking passes, hospitality amenities as well as other conventional stewardship provisions are the mechanisms that motivate donors to give to the sport organization, then it's incumbent upon those in the sport organization to provide them.

However, not all donors are motivated in the same fashion and there are those who shy away from public displays of recognition and the services that go along with it. In particular, female donors tend to be more financially protective rather than some investment-minded males. Additionally, it is more common for women to give gifts *anonymously* compared to men. "Although donors of both sexes are more likely than in the past to want to support projects that have measurable results, women have always demanded assurances that their donations will transform an institution in some respect and have a broader impact on society" (Strout 2007, p.2). Donor motivation is quite complex and while there is no consensus on this issue, sport organizations are so unique compared to other non-profit charities that research in fundraising must be examined separately.

While specific empirical research continues to evolve, there has been disagreement among the academic community as to the various *research designs* that have been utilized to study the phenomenon concerning the effects of intercollegiate athletics on fundraising. For example, a meta-analysis study conducted by Martinez et al. found that after nearly three decades of research regarding intercollegiate athletics and fundraising, all of those studies "failed to generate generalizable knowledge" (2010, p.1). However, this specific meta-analysis found that the alumni status of the donor was a significant factor. Additionally, the researchers concluded that one of the significant *implications for practice* was that an element of care should be considered to help develop and ultimately cultivate these new donors (Martinez et al. 2010). Care is a noteworthy and/or operative word. Thus, one can infer that the *expression of care* would be carried out on a personal level that focuses on their attitudes, opinions and values.

As expressed in Chapter 5, finding the *true motivation* doesn't come from a website, an article, or a spreadsheet; the only true reliable resource is the donor themselves. Through honest communication with your donors on an individualized basis, you are positioned to find the true motivating factors as well as an opportunity to let your donors know that their involvement is respected and you are able to appropriately customize stewardship provisions to reflect their needs. Once the true motivation of a donor is understood, then the use of technology as a tool to connect, manage and ultimately *protect* that information is justified.

FURTHER READING

Bee, C. C. and Kahle, L. R. (2006) "Relationship marketing in sports: A functional approach", *Sport Marketing Quarterly*, 15, 102–110.

Billing, J. E., Holt, D. and Smith, J. (1985) *Athletic fundraising: Exploring the motives behind donations*, Chapel Hill, NC: University of North Carolina Press.

Birkholz, Joshua M. (2008) *Fundraising Analytics*, Hoboken, NJ: John Wiley & Sons Inc.

Bravo, G. A. (2004) "An investigation of stakeholder influence and institutional pressures on budget strategies of high school athletic departments", Ohio State University, available at http://search.proquest.com/docview/305139790?accountid=2909 (accessed 01/31/12).

Gladden, J. M., Mahoney, D.F. and Apostolopoulou, A. (2005) "Toward a better understanding of college athletic donors: What are the primary motives?" *Sport Marketing Quarterly*, 14, 18–30.

Grimes, P. W. and Chressanthis, G. A. (1994) "Alumni contributions to academics: The role of intercollegiate sports and NCAA sanctions", *American Journal of Economics & Sociology*, 53, 27–41.

Humphreys, B. R. and Mondello, M. (2007) "Intercollegiate athletic success and donations at NCAA division I institutions", *Journal of Sport Management*, 21, 265–280.

Mahony, D. F., Gladden, J. M. and Funk, D. C. (2003) "Examining athletic donors at NCAA division I institutions", *International Sports Journal*, 7 (1) 9–27.

Martinez, J., Stinson, J., Kang, M. and Jubenville, C. (2010) "Intercollegiate athletics and institutional fundraising: A meta-analysis", *Sport Marketing Quarterly*, 19 (1) 36–47.

Staurowsky, E. J. (1996) "Women and athletic fund raising: Exploring the connection between gender and giving", *Journal of Sport Management*, 10 (4).

Stinson, J. L. and Howard, D. R. (2008) "Winning does matter: Patterns in private giving to athletic and academic programs at NCAA institutions", *Sport Management Review* 11 (1) 1–20.

Tsiotsou, R. (2006) "Investigating differences between female and male athletic donors: A comparative study", *International Journal of Nonprofit and Voluntary Sector Marketing*, 11 (3) 209–223.

Verner, M. E. (1996) "Developing women as financial donors and philanthropists: A way to enhance intercollegiate athletics opportunities", *Women in Sport & Physical Activity Journal*, 5 (1) 27–49, available at http://search.proquest.com/docview/230678216?accountid=2909 (accessed 01/31/12).

Waters, R. D. (2008) "Applying relationship management theory to the fundraising process for individual donors", *Journal of Communication Management*, 12 (1) 73–87.

Williams, K. A. (1997) *Donor focused strategies for annual giving*, Gaithersburg, MD: Aspen Publishers Inc.

APPLICATION/SKILL BUILDING EXERCISE

Exercise 1: for students

Select a college/university, a high school or a youth sport organization of your choice to examine/study. Research and determine the key personnel relative to fundraising activities. In the case of a college/university, you may consider contacting the Director of Athletic Development or Athletic Advancement. At the high school or youth level, this may be the Director of Athletics, the Youth Sport Coordinator or a Booster Club Officer such as President or Vice President. Set up a face-to-face interview or perhaps a phone interview based on their availability/schedule. Based on the chapter lesson regarding *stakeholder identification and management* as well as the *requisite resources*, keep a journal from start to finish and compile your thoughts and feelings among the following areas of inquiry. As a guidepost document their responses relative to their experience and knowledge by asking the six questions listed below. Additionally, *create* six distinctive questions of your own based on *your comprehension and interest* in the subject.

- Based on the chapter lessons, what type of fundraisers does the sport organization utilize and how would you characterize them (i.e. episodic, annual drive, individual appeals, alumni-oriented etc.)?
- What is the frequency of their fundraising activities (i.e. two times a year, three times a year, four times a year or more)?
- What kind of technology/computer systems are used to track and/or manage the fundraising activities?

- What types of communication or promotional tools are used to announce fundraising activities (i.e. phone calls, e-mail blasts, radio, TV or print advertising)?
- What strategies are used to communicate with potential donors on an individualized basis?
- Are the cultivation strategies comprehensive? Do they consider and/or are they responsive to the female donor?

Exercise 2: for practitioners

Based on the chapter lesson regarding *stakeholder identification and management* as well as the *requisite resources*, strive to answer the following areas of inquiry:

- Based on the chapter lessons, what type of fundraisers does your sport organization utilize and how would you characterize them (i.e. episodic, annual drive, individual appeals, alumni-oriented etc.)?
- What is the frequency of your fundraising activities (i.e. two times a year, three times a year, four times a year or more)?
- What kind of technology/computer systems are used to track and/or manage the fundraising activities?
- What type of communication or promotional tools are used to announce fundraising activities (i.e. phone calls, e-mail blasts, radio, TV or print advertising)?
- What strategies are used to communicate with potential donors on an individualized basis?
- Are the cultivation strategies you use comprehensive? Do they consider and/or are they responsive to the female donor?
- Based on all of your answers to the previous questions, identify and explain potential areas that could use improvement or modification? Of those areas, can you determine which aspects can be cost-effective if they were implemented?

CHAPTER 9

YOUTH/INTERSCHOLASTIC GRANTSMANSHIP OPPORTUNITIES AND APPROACHES FOR SUCCESS

The goals of this chapter are to identify and explain the rationale and processes behind successful grantsmanship opportunities among sport organizations. The strategies that are necessary to target granting agencies and other *foundations* will be covered. Additionally, specific guidelines to develop a proposal that generates successful results will be documented. Essential methods to locate and apply for grant monies that effectively communicate your needs are also the chief objectives of this chapter. The resources available relative to grantsmanship among the majority of colleges and universities in the United States are rather ample. Thus, the focus of this chapter will be on youth and high school sport programs, which in comparison don't necessarily have the highly advanced resources. While grants do not provide the *volume* of financial support as other areas, they do serve as a terrific potential source of fundraising revenue.

As has been documented in the previous chapters, understanding the contemporary dynamics and challenges associated with successful fundraising is a required skill set that sport administrators must possess in today's society. The key concepts to comprehend and appreciate are that whether you are a youth sport administrator, a high school athletic director or an officer within an athletic development department at a college or university, economic trends such as inflation combined with conceivable budget cuts, increased competition for gifts and donations as well as other foreseeable and unforeseeable financial obstacles will never go away. Money is needed to sustain quality sports programming and as such, the committed sport fundraiser, regardless of their position within the industry, must be knowledgeable, creative and resourceful in identifying and maximizing all current and potential revenue streams.

As previously detailed in Chapter 6, many communities in which sport programs exist have a very compelling anti-tax mindset. Similarly, many communities in the United States have concerns relative to *over-commercialization* among our public education institutions. Judicious evaluation of the advantages or disadvantages of allowing corporate sponsorship messages must be aligned with the mission and beliefs of the school and community. In many areas of the United States, especially in the inner cities and rural areas, they aren't even afforded the opportunities that derive from corporate partnerships due to their geographic location and socioeconomic status. Why would a large corporate business want to sponsor the sports programs of a poor rural community that is underprivileged and has a low population density? Based on experience, ordinarily, they don't. Yet, sports participation rates, while modest in comparison to larger communities, still continue to escalate in these areas of the United States. This is exactly where the notion of grantsmanship is warranted for those sport administrators who work in these communities.

For example, in Vinton County, Ohio, the school system has been the beneficiary of numerous grants. Located in southeastern Ohio within a region referred to as *rural Appalachia*, Vinton County has produced many successful sport teams and athletes. However, the challenges relative to fundraising are limiting based on its geographic location, lack of business and industry as well as infrastructure. Distressingly, Vinton County, among other rural school districts who work hard to sustain school athletic programs and youth sport organizations, is passing on participation fees to the citizens that can least afford to pay them. Tough choices are made in circumstances like these.

Moreover, based on experience as well as research, students who do not participate in extracurricular activities such as sports are more likely to engage in risky behaviors such as drinking alcohol, smoking tobacco or using drugs. They are more likely to become teen parents, drop out of school before their senior year and to have been arrested than those who spend time participating in sports and other extracurricular activities. Some of the money needed to provide these student athletes a positive environment where they can learn the values of teamwork, self-sacrifice, discipline and perseverance can be obtained through grants thus grantsmanship, is a skill set that sport administrators must possess in today's society. Therefore, learning how to start this process is the rationale of this chapter section.

LOCATING AND CATEGORIZING GRANT OPPORTUNITIES

In brief, grants are quite different than bank loans because grantees are not expected to repay the money that is awarded; instead, they are expected to report on the progress of the programs being funded as a type of stewardship. Obtaining a grant will take some significant research and the Internet as a searching tool is a good mechanism and can produce some sizeable results. Therefore, categorically breaking down grant opportunities prior to searching and locating granting agencies is a good fundamental start. Sport organizations at the youth and interscholastic levels can direct their efforts and categorize grants among the following three areas:

- government granting agencies
- corporate granting agencies
- sport-related granting agencies.

The United States government has an extensive list of grants with the *Catalog of Federal Domestic Assistance*, otherwise known as the acronym C.F.D.A. This catalog provides a full listing and descriptions of all federal programs available to state and local governments, federally recognized Indian tribal governments, United States territories as well as domestic, public, private-profit and non-profit organizations, institutions and individuals. The C.F.D.A., as of 2011, contains 2179 federal assistance programs. Additionally, the top five issuing agencies as of 2011 are as follows:

1 Department of Health and Human Services (36%)
2 Department of the Interior (21%)
3 Department of Agriculture (20%)
4 Department of Education (13%)
5 Department of Justice (10%)

Therefore, as a youth sport or an interscholastic athletic organization, it makes reasonable sense to narrow the agencies from five down to two or possibly three. The Department of Health and Human Services as well as the Department of Education are certainly aligned with sports/athletics and should be targeted to start. The guidelines and criteria these granting agencies have in supporting sports or athletic-related activities will take some thorough investigation and careful study.

The *best-practice strategy* at this point is to narrow the list even more by locating the grants/agencies that best match the mission and goals of your sport organization. That's why at the outset of this textbook the significant *prerequisites* were illustrated in Chapter 1, covering the development of a well-defined mission statement as well as introspective goals and objectives crafted through the *SMART procedure*. The importance of these prerequisites cannot be overestimated.

A key element to appreciate with government grants is that they won't allow you to contact them to influence the grant evaluation process, compared to corporate or sport-related foundations. In fact, constantly trying to build empathy to sway your case with a government grant representative would be regarded as unethical behavior. Overall, government grantors are very explicit about the types of projects they will fund and how the application proposal should be formatted. In this instance, make sure you follow all guidelines and directions to the letter. If it asks for twenty pages maximum with detailed font sizes and margin widths, that's exactly how it should be submitted.

CORPORATE GRANTING AGENCIES AND FOUNDATIONS

When it comes to locating granting agencies and foundations among the corporate world, careful analysis of the mission and objectives of your sport organization must be carried out and should be in alignment with the criteria and/or guidelines of the corporate foundation. As was previously mentioned, two of the primary differences between a government granting agency and a corporate granting agency or foundation can be found first in the way in which the application proposal is formatted and second, in the level of communication and potential influence you may have on the proposal evaluation process. In many instances, corporations are a bit more benevolent and/or lenient when it comes to talking with and establishing camaraderie with their grant agents.

Corporate foundations such as the *General Mills Foundation* are looking to make an impact on the communities in which they are supporting, not just necessarily the sports/athletics programs that exist in those communities. For example, the General Mills Foundation, in partnership with the American Dietetic Association Foundation and the President's Council on Physical Fitness, developed the Champions for Healthy Kids grant program and awards fifty grants of $10,000 each annually to community-based groups that develop creative ways to help youth adopt a balanced diet and a physically active lifestyle. The Vinton County Schools in McArthur Ohio was one of the fifty grant recipients in the late 1990s. The grant money went to replacing old and outdated physical education equipment, purchasing health and nutrition educational curriculum materials, and new cardiovascular and weight training equipment to promote physical fitness among approximately 600 youth in the area. One of the key components to securing the grant was the coordination and cooperation of needs between the athletics, health and physical education departments, and youth groups. Moreover, the rapport that was developed between Vinton County faculty and the agents from the General Mills Foundation facilitated the process of obtaining the grant.

In general, the majority of grants, including those from federal granting agencies as well as sport-related granting agencies, accept proposals that integrate the needs of students, youth and other community members, not just *athletics-only* requests. In fact, proposals that address sports- or athletics-only needs usually don't get funded unless they incorporate community and/or instructional needs as well. For example, if the need is for new athletic equipment or perhaps for a new facility or a renovation type capital project, proposals that are most effective in getting grant monies will document the usage patterns among multiple participants in order to demonstrate to the granting agency the size and/or volume of the impact it has made on the community as a whole.

Therefore, documenting usage patterns can be carried out among user groups that include, but are not limited to, the following:

- girls' and boys' varsity sports teams
- girls' and boys' non-varsity sports teams
- school physical education classes
- special education classes
- intramural programs
- recreation and community youth sport programs.

Documenting the usage patterns among these user groups and the cooperation between and among these user groups will definitely be looked upon much more favorably by corporate granting agencies and foundations. Moreover, proposals that also demonstrate their *cost-effectiveness*, in simultaneously keeping their administrative and overhead expenditures low in relation to the number of youth served, get looked upon more favorably by corporate granting agencies and foundations as well. Overall, corporate granting agencies and foundations, like the General Mills Foundation, want to get the most value for their dollar by having a *comprehensive impact* on a community in terms of supporting the nutrition and physical activity programs from a holistic perspective.

SPORT-RELATED GRANTING AGENCIES AND FOUNDATIONS

When it comes to locating granting agencies and foundations among sport-related organizations, similar to the General Mills Foundation examples provided previously, the mission and objectives of your sport organization need to be in alignment with the criteria and/or guidelines of the sport-related foundation. Additionally, just like corporate granting agencies, the grants from sport-related agencies can contain an assortment of criteria, target audiences and expectations that are quite specific to their guidelines.

For instance, if construction of a new baseball field or basketball court is being proposed, these sport-related foundations may have specific criteria that state in order to be considered, fifty percent of the total cost of the project must be obtained from *matching funds* and/or secured in-kind sources. Specifically, the *NFL Grassroots Field Grant Program* assists low to moderate income areas that surround an NFL franchise with a choice of two grant opportunities. The first is the *general field support* that has a cap of $50,000 and is intended to finance projects distinct from the football surface such as bleachers, press box, lights, concession stands etc. The second is the *field surface grant* that has a cap of $200,000 that will match the cost and installation of new synthetic field surfaces or $100,000 that will match the cost and installation of natural grass/sod field surfaces. This particular grant is aimed at the assistance of the capital expenditure for football field surface installation *only* and does not cover future field maintenance. Furthermore, an expectation for the $100,000 field surface grant is that "a minimum five-year maintenance plan and corresponding financial budget must be provided in order to demonstrate that the applying organization will maintain the field despite projected wear and tear and potential overuse by youth sports participants" (The NFL Youth Football Fund 2011, p.3).

The proposal and review processes are designed to make sure that the capital improvements to install new football fields or to renovate older fields will have a revenue stream of significant funds from the community, to support ongoing maintenance needed to sustain the use of the fields over the long term. In general, sport administrators need to be aware of these opportunities as well as the specific criteria and guidelines so that they can appropriately plan, organize and rally support from the community and apply for these sport-related grants. In the end analysis, it all starts with the mission statement and goals/ objectives of the sport organization as a prerequisite.

All three areas – government granting agencies, corporate granting agencies and sport-related granting agencies – should be pursued as potential revenue sources. Once categorized, an additional resource that can be a valuable tool in locating grants and is probably considered the best place to start your search is the *Foundation Center* and their website is http://foundationcenter.org. This website lists multiple foundations of all types and has within the site a search engine that makes narrowing down the choices very user-friendly. Once located, the Foundation Center's search results list all of the types, application procedures as well as links to the specific foundation websites as well. After the search has produced and categorized a significant number of granting agencies and foundations, the next step is to develop a grant proposal and the essential elements that are needed for success.

DEVELOPING A GRANT PROPOSAL FORMAT AND STRATEGY

As has been examined, grants can come in a variety of arrangements with variable criteria and guidelines. Being equipped with this knowledge prior to taking the time and effort to submit application proposals is a key strategy to undertake if you want your grant request to have a chance of being approved. While a significant portion of time needs to be spent researching, locating and categorizing grant opportunities, a similar amount of time needs to be devoted to understanding those agencies or foundations *before* you even start the grant-writing process. In coaching sports, *scouting* an opponent and then preparing a *game-plan* in advance of the actual game is analogous to this part of grantsmanship. The scouting and game-planning part of grantsmanship involves, but is not limited to, the following *who, what, where, when, why* and *how* components:

- Who: ascertaining *who* specifically will be reviewing the application proposal is important. Will it be reviewed by an individual or a team of critics? Then, if it is a corporate foundation or sport-related foundation, make contact with an agent or group of representatives and attempt to get copies of previous proposals that were funded by the agency in order to get a sense of what they are looking for.
- What: make certain *what* exactly the agency or foundation wants in return for the funds. Money always has strings attached; therefore, do they want basic updates on how the money is being used? Are they seeking positive publicity? Be able to determine what they want out of it and make sure you have the resources to meet those terms.
- Where: determine *where* you will obtain the necessary resources if they require it. If you are applying for an *NFL Grassroots Field Surface Grant*, you will need a five-year maintenance plan. Therefore, identifying partners, volunteers, donors as well as internal and external resources is vital so you can demonstrate to them that their money isn't being wasted. Overall, they want an assurance from the sport organization that the capital project has a plan in place to sustain the necessary upkeep for the field now and in the future.
- When: figure out *when* all application proposal materials need to be submitted or when deadline dates need to be observed. Do they allow online applications or do they require physical mailings? A postmark date is much different to an arrival or delivery deadline.
- Why: research the granting agency or foundation to determine *why* they are offering money. Is it based on geographic factors? Is it based on the financial demographics of the community (i.e. low-income rural, low-income inner city)? Make sure you understand the eligibility requirements; it's a complete waste of time if the granting agency only considers application proposals from rural communities and yours is an inner-city community and vice-versa.

- How: *how* can you demonstrate to the agency or foundation that the community at large understands the importance of your sport organization and supports the proposed project? Consider collecting testimonials, letters of support, or perhaps local press stories documenting support. In general, working with a team of key stakeholders who can help determine if:
  - A The grant opportunity is a *good fit* for your sport organization's mission/goals.
  - B There are adequate resources to put together an effective proposal.
  - C Key points are addressed and all information requested is provided. On the other hand, if any additional information is not asked for, it is best to leave it out.

Historically, grant proposals have been viewed as a communication mechanism that conveys the desires of the sport organization, states the significance for the proposed funding, and illustrates the widespread support of the sport organization to the grantor. Grant proposals, especially at the youth and interscholastic levels, generally follow a standard format that can include, but is not limited to, the following sections.

Cover letter, Abstract or Executive Summary

This part of the documentation introduces the grantee to the grantor and contains brief historical information about the sport organization and the community.

Presenting the sport organizations case on the need for funding

This part of the documentation generally includes a narrative about the sport organization, the community and populations to be served, the need for funding and how the funds address the need.

Mission Statement, objectives and benefits to the target population

This part of the documentation includes the mission statement of the sport organization as well as the goals and objectives of all the programs and services the organization provides for the athletes/youth development and/or well-being. The description should also identify the total numbers of youth being served as well as address the change you seek to accomplish from the project in terms of learning, growth or achievement.

Budget Presentation

This provides a rationale and justification for the expenses that the grant money will go towards. Depending on the type of grant request, this can include personnel expenses, such as salaries, and operating expenses, such as maintenance costs, equipment costs, transportation costs, utility costs and the like.

Messages of Support and Appendices

This part of the documentation can include items such as letters, printed out e-mail memos, testimonials or even newspaper articles that display community support for the proposed project from members of the sport organization such as athletes, coaches, parents, or from other groups such as community leaders, school leaders/administrators and local agencies. Appendices are any other type of documentation that is required by the grantor. For example, items such as audited documents describing the percentage of the population that qualifies for free lunch, audited financial statements or proof of insurance documents might be pertinent supplemental information for the grantor.

While having a formatting strategy in place is a key factor in successful grantsmanship, there are some potential pitfalls to avoid in the process that can possibly develop over time. First, while the needs of the sport organization have been clearly identified and the appropriate resources, tools and internal and external support to make it all work are in place, caution must be observed in terms of how the *style* of writing the application proposal is organized. In today's society, grant proposals are often a collaborative or *shared responsibility* and as such, are written by multiple authors or writers.

For instance, within an interscholastic athletic program, the athletic director may be responsible for writing the narrative for the section involving the mission statement, objectives and benefits to the target population. Simultaneously, the school district treasurer or business manager may be the author of the budget presentation section and the president of the athletic booster club may be responsible for writing the narrative on booster membership, external support and collecting letters of support and other testimonials. This arrangement of multiple writers can become problematic and awkward if there is not a designated *primary writer* or editor. While the concept of assigning tasks to multiple people can strengthen collaboration and teamwork, ultimately, when putting all of the sections together that is required by the grantor, there needs to be one person who can unite all of the varying writing styles into one consistent tone. Otherwise, this can lead to the proposal being rejected or sent back by the grantor for revision.

The second potential hazard to avoid is within the concept of *mission drift*. Mission drift is a short- or long-term condition whereby an organization becomes so preoccupied with its internal issues that it loses sight of its overall mission (Grace 1997). In general, fundraising as an all-inclusive term must focus on the needs the sport organization is providing, not on the needs of the sport organization itself. Therefore, in this instance, the priorities and all of the activities associated with meeting the needs of student athletes and other key stakeholders within the community changes toward procedures aimed at controlling internal conflicts. In looking at booster clubs as an example, *turnover* in the key administrative positions such as booster club president, vice-president, treasurer or secretary is a fact of life at the interscholastic level. The people who hold these positions are volunteering their time and effort and balance it with their full-time jobs and other commitments in most cases. Thus, when faced with all of the fundraising projects, including grant proposal writing, it can become overwhelming. If a key booster member's term expires or they decide to resign, the new person filling in the position must be apprised of the mission of the sport organization and what is expected of them. If there is a disconnect regarding what the person is doing and what is expected of them, then that is clearly a communication problem. If the new booster officer is expected to participate in grant-writing initiatives, then that must not only be documented, but clearly transmitted to them. If expectations are not expressed appropriately, then stress escalates, communication deteriorates and human resources are wasted because too much attention is sidetracked to worrying about or quarreling over who is responsible and as a result, the important tasks are neglected (Grace 1997).

Another type of mission drift that should be avoided at all costs is the attempt by a grantee to conform to the grantor's criteria and guidelines to such an extent that they claim to be something that they actually aren't. Referred to as *mission creep* in many fundraising circles, this implies overstating the goals and objectives of the sport organization beyond its original mission. Essentially, the allure of money can distort reality, and some sport organizations may claim to provide programs or services for student athletes when they actually don't. This kind of misrepresentation of the facts can culminate in the grantor demanding the money be returned and the reputation of the sport organization being severely tainted.

Thus, the significant aspect to remember here is that regardless of the money, you must be true to who you are and what you are all about. The stakeholders of the sport organization are the end users of the grant money. It is unethical and irrational to take such a risk to create documents that either exaggerate the truth or are complete nonsense, in order to pursue funding for funding's sake. In the end analysis, a sport organization should say *no* to funding opportunities or programs that do not align with their mission, otherwise they can jeopardize their reputation as well as their ability to accumulate grant money over the long term.

Once the proposal has been submitted, the time in between proposal submissions, the review process by the grantee and the conferring of the grant can often take months. It is prudent to utilize this *downtime* to submit alternate proposals to other grantees among the different categories previously outlined. In other words, *don't put all your eggs in one basket*. If your sport organization does obtain a grant, in all likelihood your organization will receive a personal phone call announcing the positive news. If not, a rejection letter will usually arrive unannounced in the mail. If you receive a rejection, it is not the end of the world. Potential reasons your proposal was rejected could be as simple as it arrived after the deadline date or perhaps there was something lacking in one of the content areas such as the *budget presentation*. Hypothetically speaking, perhaps there wasn't enough supporting documentation from the community or perhaps the link between the objectives of the sport organization and the health concerns of the community wasn't united enough for their liking. As was previously mentioned, the General Mills Foundation wanted to make a significant impact on improving both the physical activity levels of the youth population in Vinton County *and* their nutritional health from a holistic perspective. As you research, you will find that many foundations' priorities will be focused more on linking the physical activity programs to specific health concerns, for example improving the health of rural teenage youth as a proactive measure to fight obesity, improving the health of inner-city youth through sports and physical fitness programs, or lowering the rates of diabetes or heart disease among at-risk populations.

Being proactive and professional by following up with the grantee, keeping the conversation positive and pleasant, and trying to find out the reasons why your sport organization was rejected is advised. In the end, your sport organization should utilize this feedback and apply the lessons learned to your next proposal. Most successful grants that get funded are those that focus on programs that facilitate systematic change which connects the health concerns of the community. Therefore, if you are a youth sport organization looking for funding, then it behooves your leader or director to create partnerships. This means connecting your needs with those of the local school district's athletics and/or physical education programs and the local health departments within the community at large. As a result, if the health concern is fighting childhood obesity, then combining the resources, skills and expertise among all areas as well as rallying support to have all parties involved working cooperatively is the best approach to take when trying to obtain grants. From a planning perspective, decide to create a multi-disciplinary team consisting of physical educators, certified nutritionists as well as behavior modification experts to help design specific program components to fight childhood obesity. Then, this team should target underserved and/or disadvantaged populations, such as groups like rural Appalachians, who suffer disproportionately from diseases directly related to obesity, poor nutrition and inactivity. It is also wise to reach out and partner with neighboring schools, community centers and youth sport programs in poor neighborhoods and community health organizations that serve these target populations.

In terms of program organization, hypothetically, the parties involved could agree that your youth sport organization will provide the necessary sports equipment and coaches while the school provides the sport facilities/playing fields, and the health department provides the nutritionists and volunteers to serve healthy food. Through this type of orientation and attention to detail, this can help make your grant proposal more competitive and improve the chances of being funded by the grant agency or foundation.

FUNDAMENTAL GRANT-WRITING ADVICE

Consideration of the grant review process can be daunting; however, knowing what reviewers are looking for in the proposal is crucial to getting your sport organization funded. The three fundamental writing suggestions listed below include, but are not limited to:

1. Reviewers expect you to follow the guidelines. If they ask for a format of Times New Roman in 12-point font, the proposal *must* adhere to those writing guidelines.
2. Reviewers don't like surprises. As previously mentioned, if the format is modified or inconsistent, the guidelines are disregarded, and there is required information missing from the proposal, this can result in denial and a forthcoming rejection letter.
3. Reviewers are detail-oriented. Ensuring that the spelling, grammar, format, and overall precision of your proposal are appropriately written speaks volumes about your sport organization. Make sure your grant writing reflects these three elements because reviewers tend to fund programs that pay attention to detail in their proposal.

ESSENTIAL GRANT INFORMATION RESOURCES

Check the following websites on a regular basis to learn of current and future grant opportunities.

Suggested United States Government Websites

The U.S. Department of Education: www.ed.gov/
The U.S. Department of Health and Human Services: www.hhs.gov/

Suggested Corporate Foundation Websites

General Mills Foundation's Champions for Healthy Kids: www.generalmills.com/Responsibility/Community_Engagement/Grants.aspx

Liberty Mutual's Responsible Sports program for Youth Sports: www.responsiblesports.com/default.aspx

The Finish-Line Youth Foundation: http://www.finishline.com/store/youthfoundation/youthfoundation.jsp

Suggested Sport-Related Foundation Websites

The Baseball Tomorrow Fund: http://mlb.mlb.com/mlb/official_info/community/btf.jsp

The NFL Grassroots Field Grant Program: https://www.nflyff.org/grant_programs/grassroots

The GoGirlGo! Program: http://www.womenssportsfoundation.org/en/home/programs/gogirlgo

FURTHER READING

Adams, M. A. (2011) "Normalizing life through participation in after school activity programs: A grant proposal", California State University, Long Beach, available at http://search.proquest.com/docview/866305811?accountid=2909 (accessed 01/31/12).

Bauer, D. G. (1999) *The "how to" grants manual*, Phoenix, AZ: American Council on Education: Oryx Press.

—— (1999) *The principal's guide to writing grants*, San Francisco, CA: Jossey-Bass Publishers.

Gill, D. (2009) "Grant Helps East Texas Triathletes Club Thrive", *Triathlon Life*, 12 (2) 93, available at search.epnet.com.

Golden, S. L. (1997) *Secrets of successful grantsmanship; a guerrilla guide to raising money*, San Francisco, CA: Jossey-Bass Publishers.

Grace, K. S. (1997) *Beyond Fundraising: new strategies for non-profit innovation and investment*, New York, NY: John Wiley & Sons Inc.

Huck, T. (2005) "Participation in extracurricular activities in secondary school: What is known, what needs to be known?" *Review of Educational Research*, 57, 251–262.

Johnson, D. D. and Schilling, T. T. (2001) "Get the gold: A physical educator's guide to grant writing", *JOPERD: The Journal of Physical Education, Recreation & Dance*, 72 (3) 48–53, 58–59, available at search.epnet.com.

LA84 Foundation (aka Amateur Athletic Foundation) (2011) "Foundation grant guidelines", available at http://www.aafla.org/1gm/GRANTGUIDELINESPrinterFriendlyText.pdf (accessed 01/31/12).

Little, P. M. D., Wimer, C. and Weiss, H. B. (2007) *After school programs in the 21st century: Their potential and what it takes to achieve it*, Cambridge, MA: Harvard Family Research Project.

Rikard, G. L. (2008) "Money for the asking: Writing small grants for physical education", *Journal of Physical Education, Recreation & Dance*, 79 (6) 3–4, 15, available at http://search.proquest.com/docview/215758539?accountid=2909 (accessed 01/31/12).

Robinson, A. (2004) *Grassroots grants: An activist's guide to grant-seeking*, San Francisco, CA: Jossey-Bass Publishers.

Ross, D. (1985) *Fundraising for youth*, Colorado Springs, CO: Meriwether Publishers.

Stier, W. F. (1996) "An overview of administering competitive sports through effective marketing, fundraising and promotions", *Applied Research in Coaching & Athletics Annual*, 11 (1) 116–128.

The NFL Youth Football Fund start-page (2011) available at https://www.nflyff.org (accessed 01/31/12).

APPLICATION/SKILL BUILDING EXERCISE

Exercise applicable for both students and practitioners

Based on the chapter lesson regarding *grantsmanship*, get on the Internet and locate a granting agency among the three categories (Government Granting Agencies, Corporate Granting Agencies and

Sport-related Granting Agencies) and examine their criteria and guidelines.

As a guidepost, listed below are suggested questions that will aid you in creating your own grant proposal based on your situation. Try to answer and document the following:

Based on the chapter lesson, choose one of the agencies and make every effort to answer the *who*, *what*, *where*, *when*, *why* and *how* questions presented on pages 162–163.

Now create a proposal based on an actual or hypothetical sport organization utilizing the *format strategy* illustrated on pages 163–164. Be sure to include all five sections:

- cover letter, abstract or executive summary
- presenting the sport organization's case on the need for funding
- mission statement, objectives and benefits to the target population
- budget presentation
- messages of support and appendices.

CHAPTER 10

THE FUTURE OF SPORTS FUNDRAISING: DATA-DRIVEN METHODOLOGIES AND CURRICULUM DEVELOPMENT IN HIGHER EDUCATION

The intent of this chapter is threefold. First is to identify and explain the essential aspects of data mining and predictive analytics used in institutional fundraising and how incorporating these statistical methodologies are the future of sports fundraising. Second is to provide a fundamental synopsis of the areas in higher education where practical applications of these analytical models have been successful, and potential resources to aid in helping sport organizations apply them into their processes. Third is to provide an overview of sport administration/sport management educational programs in the United States and demonstrate how the use of technology to deliver these data methods and statistical approaches is a key component to the future as it relates to curriculum development in sport administration/sport management. A brief overview on strategies of how to bridge the gap between sport management academics and practitioners is also presented. Finally, the value of incorporating an interdisciplinary approach to curriculum development and instruction, as well as the value of this pedagogical method for delivering instruction to future generations, will be included.

How does the incorporation of data mining and predictive analytics come into play with sports fundraising? As will be demonstrated, it has everything to do with sports fundraising; it is the key to its imminent growth in the entire sport industry. Also, it should have a significant impact on sport management undergraduate and graduate curriculum development. So, what exactly are data mining and predictive analytics?

DATA MINING

Fundamentally, data mining is not a search for data, analogous to how coal mining is a search for coal. Rather, data mining is a search within a voluminous amount of data to provide information, insight and a comprehension of tendencies and/or relationships among them. Data mining applies meticulous statistical examination to large masses of data so that significant patterns and relationships, which are often buried by the sheer volume and grouping of the data, are uncovered so that judicious decisions can be made (Fuller 2002).

While data mining methodologies are an important tool in extracting trends and patterns within large volumes of data, it does not magically provide the answers that motivate the end user of the information to take a particular course of action. Therefore, while data mining can provide relationships, they are not causal relationships. Whereas in typical experimental research that utilizes inferential statistics to test a predetermined hypothesis or group of hypotheses in an attempt to find out causality, data mining is different in that the process is exploratory in construct.

As a result, data mining searches for hidden relationships and patterns in the data that can add to our knowledge about a particular situation. Therefore, it is important to note that data mining is not a simple remedy or silver bullet. When it comes to making decisions, it boils down to having an individual who understands the fundraising environment to know how to interpret which tools are of value. Hypothetically, if more knowledge about donor motivation is needed for the Associate Director of Athletic Advancement at a university, then data mining is a tool that can produce efficient results that is both time- and cost-effective. This type of statistical methodology is already used in the business industry among those in marketing, retail services, telecommunications and financial services, just to name a few. Within sport, data mining is used primarily among those involved in the gaming industry, where fantasy football or fantasy baseball is big business, and also among professional sport organizations to help sport coaches and managers make informed decisions on numerical facts rather than on gut feelings.

Data elements such as on-base percentage, number of hits and strikeouts, among others, can be used in data mining and it provides coaches and managers with a tool so that more knowledgeable decisions can be made about how to move forward with those decisions. Moreover, being armed with this knowledge has the potential to secure a competitive advantage versus the competition.

PREDICTIVE ANALYTICS

Predictive analytics encompasses a variety of statistical techniques, including data mining. It analyzes the past with the present-day facts in order to forecast the future. In other words, it incorporates and scores demographic elements in conjunction with scored behavioral elements. Reflecting back on the information presented in Chapter 4, it was illustrated that assigning a numeric value to a soft data variable can save a sport organization considerable time and money by systematically categorizing your stakeholders. This process provides categorized demographic information. For example, in the demographic category of living or deceased, you can use 1/0 fields where 1 = living and 0 = deceased. Perhaps in the demographic category of year of birth, you can use 1/0 fields where 1 = people born between 1920 and 1979 and 0 = people born between 1980 and the present. Predictive analytics has the ability to take data mining a step further by including and scoring behavioral elements about stakeholders in combination with demographic elements. Zaman explains this concept well by stating "The core element of predictive analytics is the predictor, a variable that can be measured for an individual or entity to predict future behavior. For example, a credit card company could consider age, income, gender and other demographics as predictors when issuing a credit card to determine an applicant's risk factor" (2005, p.1). Simultaneously, a credit issuing company will also consider that behavioral elements that can be scored include previous pay history, how much debt the individual has on other credit cards based on their balances, how often new credit is applied for as well as the length of their credit history, for example.

Then, the role of predictive analytics is to provide a FICO credit score. That score will allow the credit card issuer to help determine how much they are willing to risk. Will they give a person a credit line limit of $500, $1,000 or $15,000? Overall, these behavioral elements are quite important predictors, because actual behavior is better at predicting future behavior than demographic characteristics. Hypothetically speaking, just because someone has an annual income of $150,000 does not necessarily make them a good prospect for a donation for our athletic department. Perhaps they are in extreme debt and have multiple credit cards maxed out; another person who makes an annual income of $65,000 and has no debt may be more appropriate to target. As a result, data mining and predictive analytics have the capacity to improve the efficiency and effectiveness of sport fundraising. Consider the following example: as a university athletic development office, you have multiple constituents and stakeholders both internal and external to your organization. Moreover, all of these people pursue certain routines and any change in that routine is a challenge as you cultivate a relationship with them. When the time comes for an annual drive for the athletic fund, you can predict future behavior based on an understanding of their past behavior, and you can utilize this knowledge to demonstrate how much their donation has helped improve the programs and services for athletic success.

Hypothetically, let's assume a 55-year-old man is a perfect demographic match for your annual athletic fund drive, but rarely attends sporting event on your campus. Now, compare this to a 55-year-old woman who is normally outside of your core demographic, but repeatedly goes to athletic events and purchases a great deal of licensed merchandise for both her children and grandchildren. Consequently, if you sent an e-mail informing both of them about the importance of your annual athletic fund drive, who is more likely to be inclined to give a donation? The key point to understand and appreciate is that demographic information can only tell you limited information, or only a part of the picture. As previously stated, behavioral elements are quite important predictors, because actual behavior is better than demographic characteristics at predicting future behavior. Therefore, approaching the 55-year-old woman for a donation is quite obvious based on the example provided. However, many institutions in intercollegiate athletics rely heavily on demographic information and as such, it can be potentially misguiding. This example demonstrates a potential missed opportunity for a significant donation, especially if this woman was never on the radar of the athletic development office to begin with.

Overall, it certainly demonstrates the value and utility of predictive analytics in sport fundraising. Data mining and predictive analytics can be an integral part of the athletic development landscape as it allows sport organizations to be proactive about situations rather than retrospective. In other words, it means sport organizations can attempt to predict future trends rather than discovering them after they have already taken place. Additionally, there are aspects of data mining and predictive analytics that can clearly be useful for those administrators at the youth and high school levels as well. An analysis of how these statistical methodologies are successfully securing private donations and gifts of significance among institutions of higher education will be forthcoming in this chapter.

DATA MINING AND PREDICTIVE ANALYTICS IN HIGHER EDUCATION ADVANCEMENT AND PRACTICAL APPLICATIONS

The contemporary dynamics of an unstable United States economy has substantially impacted the way in which college and university advancement offices conduct their business.

Private philanthropy efforts aimed at conventional sources of support such as appreciative alumni, charitable faculty and staff and other groups of donors have grown significantly over the last thirty years. Due to economic instabilities, the appeals for these gifts are no longer a nice gesture, but rather they are critical items on the financial statements of many colleges and universities. Furthermore, the pressing need for these donations to go towards subsidizing new buildings or building renovations, technological enhancements, faculty positions, program development and student financial aid packages are just a few examples as to why fundraising is so important. Tight budgets and hiring freezes are also forcing many university advancement offices to do more with less. Fundamental data mining and predictive analytics do not have to be an expensive undertaking, and they can yield a substantial return on investment.

In a case study of ten institutions, Dan Luperchio of Johns Hopkins University created and applied a predictive analytical model based on commonly collected variables such as graduation year, gender, city, state, race, and number of children, and then created a ten-step model with a testing process (Luperchio 2009). The results of this case study were successful at all ten institutions. The wider applicability of this effective study has significant implications for those in sport fundraising. "Fundraisers will benefit from this work by using the model to generate predictive scores identifying prospects in their own alumni databases, likely to make a major gift as well as appreciating their own institutions' pattern of giving when making strategic fundraising decisions" (Luperchio 2009, p.2). Moreover, the advantage of utilizing this predictive model is that when there is an adequate amount of data, the model was able to accomplish the following:

- The model can be used to identify major prospects for a single fundraising initiative (e.g. undergraduate financial aid), for a category of related initiatives (e.g. capital projects), from an internal constituency (e.g. part-time alumni), or from a cohort (e.g. class of 1979). Similarly, the model can predict response to a particular annual fund solicitation (e.g. calendar year-end e-mail) or solicitation vehicle (e.g. direct mail) (Luperchio 2009, p.8).
- The success of this predictive analytical case study clearly has the potential to produce tangible rewards in the sport fundraising arena that are not only user-friendly (SPSS statistical products were used), but provides swift results that can be replicated.

How can this data-driven type of undertaking be accomplished on a limited amount of resources? A good beginning would be by doing some simple analyses with the tools currently utilized and then placing them into an MS Excel spreadsheet. It is a fairly safe assumption that every college athletic advancement office has some sort of computerized system for compiling, storing and organizing data. For the purposes of this example, let's postulate that Microsoft Office is the system on most athletic advancement departments' computers. MS Excel spreadsheet is a significant yet underestimated program contained in Microsoft Office.

MS Excel has an add-on type of downloadable program named XL Miner, which allows users to perform data mining applications. One of the first questions to be answered when it comes time to move forward with this type of undertaking revolves around who will truly be involved in the work of mining the data? Namely, will in-house members of the athletic advancement staff be involved and trained on how to perform data mining, will a third-party outside expert assume this role, or will there be a combination? Historically, athletic development staffing has been limited.

A cost-effective approach could be gained by being resourceful enough to reach out for free help among specific departments on campus by creating a cooperative partnership. This is a parallel approach to the one illustrated in Chapter 5 regarding feasibility studies. The advantages of this form of partnering are that it allows the athletic development department to keep their costs down while at the same time providing a meaningful learning experience for students who are studying this aspect as part of their college curriculum. This kind of cooperative research project can be valuable because many mathematics and statistics professors on college campuses have significant experience and are skilled in statistical methodology and analyses. Furthermore, the students will provide valuable labor, through the input and mining of data that the athletic advancement department deems as important variables. Overall, this can prove to be a win–win situation for everyone involved.

Another potential resource of gaining knowledge about data mining on a limited budget would be through networking and learning from others who conduct prospect research and who utilize these types of analytical tools for fundraising. National professional organizations such as the Association of Prospect Researchers for Advancement or A.R.P.A, as well as the National Association of Athletic Development Directors or N.A.A.D.D. are a decent starting point. In many instances, these professional organizations hold workshops and conferences for the members of their organizations at specific times during the year. Usually members get discounted rates for workshops and other professional development courses compared to non-members. As a result, it is up to the individual institution to determine whether or not the membership and associated workshop fees are a wise investment.

A key component to remember here is that computer proficiency is quickly becoming the norm. The ability to be skillful and manage data is the future of sport fundraising at all levels. Relevant computer applications and software programs include, but are not limited to, the following:

- SQL or Structured Query Language
- ArcGIS (Geographic Information Systems)
- Experian QAS or Quick Address Software
- MS Excel spreadsheet, graphs and charts
- MS Powerpoint, Access and Word.

Technology has redefined how we do business in the sport industry as well as within the academic world. E-mail, MS Word documents, Excel spreadsheets, pdf files, databases, software and hardware programs are now current vernacular across a wide range of disciplines, including sport administration. Proficiency with technology as well as data management systems like those examples listed above are important for professional practitioners and students alike to possess in today's society.

CURRICULUM DEVELOPMENT IN SPORT ADMINISTRATION/SPORT MANAGEMENT IN THE UNITED STATES

Sport administration and/or sport management is a relatively new concept in the academic world. In fact, Kreutzer indicates that the first sports administration program was established in 1966 at Ohio University and "The curriculum was adopted and the first students were admitted" (2000, p.66). Since 1966, the discipline of sport management as an academic field has grown significantly and according to the North American Society for Sport Management's website, as of 2011, there are 330 universities offering sport management programs in the United States (NASSM 2011).

Many interchangeable terms have been used to describe the profession, "such as sport(s) or athletic management, sport(s) business or administration, and athletic administration" (Stier 1993, p.3). This lack of agreement within its own language to describe the profession has been thoroughly debated in the research literature over the last thirty years. Simultaneously, curriculum development within sport management has been a highly debated subject as well.

Historically, when developing an undergraduate and graduate curriculum, many researchers illustrated that modifications to sport management curriculum was needed to due to the change in market conditions. Exactly how or what types of changes were needed to modify the sport management curriculum is still debated today. Overall, the lack of agreement relative to curriculum has indisputably helped identify and influence well-defined areas in this field of study. As detailed in Chapter 3, the debates and growing pains in regard to curriculum development reflect its versatility. "Taken as a whole, it has been these problems and growing pains that have helped influence and augment sports administration curriculum at all levels" (Kelley 2002, p.30). In reaction to the lack of consensus regarding curriculum among sport management programs, the National Association for Sport and Physical Education (NASPE) joined forces with the North American Society for Sport Management (NASSM) in 1993 and created the NASPE-NASSM Program Standards that specify the minimum core content for both undergraduate and graduate programs in sport management. The overall objective was to prescribe standardized content areas aimed at providing students with an essential body of knowledge needed for careers within the sport industry.

As time progressed, the 1993 standards were modified in 2000. Between 2000 and 2006, more modifications were adopted as well as the formation of task forces within the NASPE-NASSM membership to come up with an organization to standardize and regulate curriculum accreditation. By September 2007, NASPE and NASSM agreed to initiate a new accreditation organization in July 2008 named the Commission on Sport Management Accreditation (COSMA). In total, the primary objective of COSMA accreditation is through the assessment process, relative to student learning and operational outcomes that have a business orientation. Detailed study regarding the COSMA accreditation process can be obtained at http://www.cosmaweb.org/, for those interested in pursuing more detail and enrichment. Consequently, sports fundraising, despite its obvious importance in contemporary society, receives little attention in both the professional literature and coursework. Moreover, it is not listed as a student learning outcome among the COSMA objectives.

Among sport literature and educational textbooks, in most instances, sports fundraising as a topic of subject matter is relegated to a book chapter or perhaps a few pages within a book chapter. This subject is not covered in most sports management programs. While a sports fundraising class is not as common within sport management curriculums as perhaps courses titled sport finance, sport marketing, or economics of sport, in recent years there does appear to be growth in the area. Ironically, the field of sport management is the ideal location to teach this essential subject matter and as such, deserves substantial consideration for inclusion into the curriculum. Sports fundraising should be considered a key content area and should be adequately covered within the context of sport management degree programs in the United States.

Conversely, one of the biggest incongruities is the gap between the NASPE-NASSM and eventually the COSMA accreditation process and sport management programs in the United States. Currently, there happen to be more sport management programs that are not COSMA approved than those that are. An empirical study by Laird in 2003 examined the accreditation process prior to the formation of COSMA. His research findings provide insight on the perceptions of academicians who were not in agreement with accreditation compared to those who were. The study determined "significant differences in perception of the NASPE-NASSM approval process exist between academicians from programs that are approved and academicians from programs that have never applied for approval" (Laird 2003, p.213). Furthermore, "There is very little research or evidence to demonstrate that being a student from a NASPE-NASSM approved program benefits that student in taking a job in the industry" (Laird 2003, p.146). Finally, "The NASPE-NASSM approval process was created to improve the level of curriculum quality in sport management. What is not clear is whether this level of quality has been achieved" (Laird 2003, p.149).

Sport management is a versatile field of study. Additionally, the field itself is also profoundly influenced by an ever-changing marketplace: the contemporary dynamics of economic instability, inflationary conditions, inadequate allocation of resources combined with the pressure to do more things with less money are just a few examples of the industry. Therefore, "A 'one curriculum fits all' model cannot meet the needs of such a diverse industry" (Kreutzer 2000, p.72) Additionally, it is suggested by Kreutzer (2000, p.72) that "Perhaps we would better serve students who plan to pursue a career in youth, high school or college athletics by preparing them not to be athletic administrators, but rather academic administrators with a concentration in athletics".

For example, a student who aspires to become a high school director of athletics mandates a curriculum that is flexible enough to accommodate their career goal in comparison to the student who aspires to work in the marketing department of a professional sports franchise. Thus, coursework needs to be developed in an interdisciplinary fashion so that they truly understand the intricacies, politics and dynamics faced in a high school environment. When it comes time for the student to attain the required practicum, internship, co-op or work-study hours needed to graduate, those experiences should be required to have an educational module and could be carried out with, for example:

- a high school or college athletic director
- a building principal, a superintendent of schools or a college dean
- a school district's central business office or a college development or advancement office
- a high school guidance counselor or a college athletic academic services director.

Kreutzer asserts "such practical experience will serve those who wish to pursue a career in high school or college athletics far more effectively than being one of many interns in a ticket office" (2000, p.73).

In sum, the training of future athletic administrators in educational settings and the ability to fully maximize their capabilities within institutions of higher education, sport management program administrators must consider "using an educationally centered curriculum, rather than solely the business-centered curriculum suggested by the accreditation model" (Kreutzer 2000, p.66).

TECHNOLOGY DEVELOPMENT IN THE SPORT ADMINISTRATION/SPORT MANAGEMENT CURRICULUM

As was explained in Chapter 2, as the United States entered into the new millennium, new technological developments emerged and as such, we quickly entered into the age of technology which saw an explosion of people using the Internet as a social networking medium and other computer aided technologies. Prior to the 1990s, many terms such as e-mail and pdf files were non-existent. As a result, technology usage in higher education is a mandatory tool and students need to be exposed and trained to properly employ these technological enhancements. As detailed in Chapter 1, significant ways in which technology is delineating the sports world can be seen in the technological advances within the sports equipment, sport facilities and sport surface industries. Other areas include, but are not limited to, the following:

- broadcasting via the Internet and the concept of webcasting
- instant messaging and social networking sites

- licensed merchandise sales via e-commerce
- marketing and promotions via virtual signage
- web-based fundraising via computerized prospect management systems.

In a study, Hjerpe demonstrates that the lack of technology in sport management curriculum has "failed to train students to meet the expectations of employers" (2009, p.8). Consequently, her study revealed that "While students received considerable theory in their programs, they were not particularly well trained with the practical tools needed to do their daily job on the workforce" (Hjerpe 2009, p.9). Therefore, sport management academics in institutions of higher education have a responsibility to effectively train students to enter the sport industry with the skills in order to meet the technological demands.

While theory is a beneficial piece of the sport management curriculum, there needs to be an equivalent amount of practical, hands-on technological training as well. Unfortunately, there are many instances of resistance and an overall disconnect between academic researchers and practitioners. Many practitioners in the sport industry feel that the academic research in sport management is relatively perplexing and lacks application. Modest amounts of sport management research conducted by academics are actually being utilized by practitioners and as such, have intensified the gap between the two groups. This gap has been referenced by several books, articles and research studies. There needs to be a healthy bridge between sport management academicians and practitioners, and to help re-connect the two groups, options include, but are not limited to, the following three strategies:

Collaborative Projects

This is best accomplished if there are projects that can be initiated by the sport academician that would be of most benefit to the practitioners.

Hypothetically, an academician can connect and meet with a high school athletics director to inquire about their needs or a particular project that is beyond the practitioner's ability to implement, but has the potential to be of value for both the professor and high school athletic director. For example, let's assume a high school athletic director is looking to raise funds for a gymnasium renovation with a new maple floor and new bleachers. He or she may not have the time or resources to initiate an updated list of alumni to enter into an MS Excel spreadsheet, which is a key group that the athletic director wants to get involved. The sport management professor can collaborate and perhaps provide students to assist with the project. This collaborative project not only helps the practitioner in the eventual solicitation of alumni, but also helps the sport management professor and his students get hands-on experience with a fundraising project. With proper oversight of the student's work by both parties, this can be a win–win situation.

Guest Lecturing and Job Shadow Opportunities

One of the key reasons why there is a gap between sport management academics and practitioners is a lack of effective communication because they come from distinctly different cultures. Therefore, opportunities to experience each other's worlds might be a great way to bridge the gap that exists. Inviting practitioners to deliver a presentation on current events or the status of their part of the sport industry to a classroom full of sport management students is recommended. Alternatively, if the physical location of the college campus is too great a distance for the practitioner to travel, perhaps video-conferencing technology can be carried out so both academics and students have an opportunity to interact and speak with sport industry practitioners. On the other hand, having the sport management professor job shadow the practitioner or perhaps having some sport management students job shadow practitioners in the sport organization can ultimately help improve communication and be beneficial for everyone involved.

Symposium events and social gatherings/networking

This is a great opportunity to bridge the gap by having a meeting or a conference that would include sport management academic scholars, sport management students and sport industry practitioners for social interaction, networking, and an opportunity to dialogue/share ideas.

The future outlook is bright if sport management academics and practitioners can come together and collaborate with one another. More partnerships and projects aimed at satisfying both academic research and practical applications will eventually have benefits for each group in addition to the most important stakeholders of all … the students!

SEEKING CURRICULAR BALANCE THROUGH AN INTERDISCIPLINARY APPROACH IN SPORT MANAGEMENT

An interdisciplinary approach to education is becoming more and more popular from early childhood to graduate level pedagogy. There are both advocates and cynics of the interdisciplinary approach. Critics point out that the approach is too time consuming. The growing pains associated with its time consuming nature, and getting collaboration from various fields such as sport management, business, marketing, statistics and mathematics, can appear daunting. But in the end analysis, it is worth the effort to advance pedagogical creativity, communication and critical thinking within the sport management curriculum. Educational leaders in the field of sport administration have illustrated that the field of study "revolves around an interdisciplinary or multidisciplinary approach" (Stier 1993, p.3). Regrettably, there are some colleges and universities that claim their pedagogical approach is interdisciplinary when in reality this isn't necessarily the case. In college athletics, the new standards by which athletic directors assess their effectiveness in contemporary society involve, but are not limited to, the following aspects:

- television broadcasting rights agreements
- negotiating concessions operations contracts with third parties
- advertising revenue and corporate sponsorship packages
- leveraging seating through priority points programs
- logo/apparel licensing contracts
- facility upgrades and luxury box seating.

Understandably, all of the components listed above are important to any sport administrator.

As has been illustrated in Chapter 4, one of the primary objectives of this textbook rests within the concept that despite the differences between the fundraising activities carried out at the college level compared to the youth and high school levels, there are fundamental principles, techniques, strategies, models and guidelines to effectively plan, organize, communicate, direct, implement, manage and evaluate that are applicable at all levels. Consequently, the contemporary pedagogical approach among sport management programs in the United States is that they are all about the core business functions and other bottom-line elements. It is recommended that an equivalent emphasis should be placed on educating the next generation of sport administrators to understand and appreciate the mission-driven values of education as well as examine and comprehend the environment in which the athletic department shares with other departments on campus. Kreutzer clearly makes the point when he states:

> Understanding how these elements fit into the mission of a college or high school athletics department, however, is of equal or greater importance. Sport management students who stand awestruck at the sight of a multimillion dollar campus athletic facility whose primary purpose is to glamorize the recruiting process for a limited number of blue-chip recruits find it difficult to answer when asked if there could be another way to allocate those same resources to better serve the mission of the institution. Do sport management students even understand the process through which educational institutions identify their missions? Strategic planning, a process that takes vision and mission and translates them into action, is a critical management function as fundamental to organizational success as marketing or finance.
>
> (2000, p.66)

Thus, curriculum should reflect these educational aims and objectives by balancing instruction about revenue generating techniques, essential business objectives and ROI, with education centered mission-driven methods of instruction. In other words, the fundamental line of reasoning to understand at this point is that students are already entering into the sport industry knowledgeable about the business side of managing an athletic department, but do they really understand the role athletics plays in the mission of the university?

In sum, implementing a balanced methodology of delivering sport management curriculum is truly the aim of an interdisciplinary approach. Without an interdisciplinary approach, the ability to answer or perhaps solve the problems associated with the unethical and, in some cases, illegal practices of academic misconduct, gender inequity, recruiting violations as well as fundraising fraud and embezzlement among others will continue to elude us. In the end, these issues will sporadically escalate and as a result, continue to alienate the athletic department from the rest of the campus.

INTERDISCIPLINARY APPROACHES TO CURRICULUM DEVELOPMENT IN SPORT MANAGEMENT AND HIGHER EDUCATION

A basic definition of an interdisciplinary curriculum is that it is arranged to analyze a dynamic concept and/or field of study by collecting and linking ideas from multiple disciplines. Curriculum development in sport management needs to be augmented so that this type of approach can support teaching and inspiring sport administrators of the future. Many current issues, problems and questions regarding trends such as lack of funding for athletics, gender inequity, donor motivations, predictive analytics or even economics of American culture creates a wide scope of inquiry. The objective of interdisciplinary approaches is to identify links and initiate alliances with scholars and/or practitioners who have diverse educational backgrounds, but similar interests. The essential argument to be understood and appreciated is that sport is so complex it requires multiple academic and pragmatic approaches to analyze it. Newell and Klein succinctly point out the merits of this approach; while they are not specifically referring to the field of sport management, the positive implications are apparent:

> The realization that many important problems do not fit neatly into traditional disciplinary domains is as commonplace as beliefs that boundaries are blurring and that knowledge is becoming increasingly interdisciplinary. No one method or approach can adequately deal with the problems of population, health, environmental pollution, crime and hunger. Multidisciplinary and client-based problems are also driving the need for structures orthogonal to traditional divisions.
>
> (1996, p.163)

In other words, there are some problems, relationships and/or other phenomena in sport management that appear to be more appropriate to view from a variety of perspectives rather than the scope of one curricular lens. While the merits of this approach in sport management appear to be logical, there are critics outside of sport who condemn the methodology by saying it is too time consuming; it can also be perceived as atypical and too far away from the mainstream, and characterized as not having a wide appeal due to a lack of expertise. While these perceptions are authentic, it appears that they could demonstrate more of a presumptuous resistance to the approach. Overall the approach must be well understood by all and as a plus, cost-effective as well.

In conclusion, sports fundraising is a fundamental piece of the sport management puzzle. There are definite links between traditional disciplines that can include, but certainly are not limited to, the following:

- curriculum and instruction
- educational leadership
- instructional design and technology
- computer science/database management
- operations and business analytics
- higher education.

Overall, the list above is just a small sample of the potential areas among traditional educational disciplines that could be utilized in an interdisciplinary fashion. As we move forward into the future, an interdisciplinary approach within sport management curriculum has the potential to create a better understanding of the intricacies, politics and dynamics within the sport industry.

FURTHER READING

Benford, R. D. (2007) "The college sports reform movement: Reframing the 'edutainment' industry", *Sociological Quarterly*, 48, 1–28.

Birkholz, J. M. (2008) *Fundraising Analytics*, Hoboken, NJ: John Wiley & Sons Inc.

Havenstein, H. (2006) "Celtics turn to data analytics tool for help pricing tickets", *Computerworld*, 43.

Henze, L. (2010) "Using statistical modeling to increase donations", available at https://www.blackbaud.com/files/resources/downloads/WhitePaper_TargetAnalytics_StatisticalModeling.pdf (accessed 01/31/12).

Hjerpe, K. L. (2009) "The absence of technology in undergraduate sport management curriculum and its relationship to intercollegiate and professional athletics", Robert Morris University, available at http://search.proquest.com/docview/305167633?accountid=2909 (accessed 01/31/12).

Kelley, D. J. (2002) "An analysis of differences between gender, experience and school size regarding the responsibilities of interscholastic athletic directors", Ohio University, available at http://search.proquest.com/docview/305523272?accountid=2909 (accessed 01/31/12).

LeBlanc, L. A. and Rucks, C. T. (2009) "Data mining of university philanthropic giving: Cluster-discriminant analysis and pareto effects", *International Journal of Educational Advancement*, 9 (2) 64–82.

Letter, G. J., Drane, D. D. and Orejan, J. (2008) "Describing sport management practitioners information technology (IT) competence and training needs", *Sport Journal*, 11 (1).

Luperchio, D. (2009) *Data mining and predictive modeling in institutional advancement: How ten schools found success*, Washington, D.C.: Council for Advancement and Support of Education.

Meer, J. and Rosen, H. S. (2008) "The impact of athletic performance on alumni giving: An analysis of microdata", *Economics of Education Review*, 28 (3) 287–294.

Newell, W. H. and Klein, J. T. (1996) "Interdisciplinary studies into the 21st century", *Journal of General Education*, 45 (2) 152–169.

Rogerson, L. J. (2006) "Interdisciplinary collaboration: Facilitating the road to performance", University of Alberta, available at http://search.proquest.com/docview/304961398?accountid=2909 (accessed 01/31/12).

Rosandich, T. J. (2001) "Information Technology for Sports Management", *Sport Journal*, 4 (2), available at http://www.thesportjournal.org/article/information-technology-sports-management (accessed 01/31/12).

Schmidt, J. C. (2001) "Mining philanthropic data: Models for predicting alumni/us giving at a medium-sized public master's university", University of Minnesota, available at http://search.proquest.com/docview/304705037?accountid=2909 (accessed 01/31/12).

Spivey, L. M. (2008) "Division I athletics directors and university presidents: A comparison of sport-related values", *Educational Leadership*, available at http://search.proquest.com/docview/250809284?accountid=2909 (accessed 01/31/12).
Thompson, L. A. (2010) "Data mining for higher education advancement: A study of eight North American college and universities", North Dakota State University, available at http://search.proquest.com/docview/822168028?accountid=2909 (accessed 01/31/12).
Wilson, L. S. (2008) "Examining technology utilization in sport management curricula and teaching", Doctoral Dissertation, Ohio State University, available at http://etd.ohiolink.edu/view.cgi?acc_num=osu1213226129 (accessed 01/31/12).
Wylie, P. B. (2010, May 3) "The tough job of bringing in new alumni donors", available at http://cooldata.wordpress.com/2010/05/03/the-tough-job-of-bringing-in-new-alumni-donors/ (accessed 01/31/12).
—— (2004) *Data mining for fundraisers*, Washington, DC: Council for Advancement and Support of Education.
Wylie, P. B. and Sammis, J. (2008) "Does data mining really work for higher education fundraising? A study of the results of predictive models built for five higher education institutions", available at http://www.case.org/Documents/Books/29502/Does_Data_Mining_Really_Work.pdf (accessed 01/31/12).

APPLICATION/SKILL BUILDING EXERCISE

Exercise 1: for students

Select a college/university that has an educational program in Sport Management/Sport Administration. Research and determine who the key personnel are relative to the academic programming. Additionally, within the same college/university, attempt to contact the Director of Athletic Development or Athletic Advancement. In both instances, try and set up a face-to-face interview or perhaps a phone interview based on their availability/schedule. Based on the chapter lesson regarding curriculum development, attempt to answer the following areas of inquiry. As a guidepost, document their responses relative to their experience and knowledge about curriculum development. Ask the sport management academic program administrator the four questions listed below. Additionally, create four distinctive questions of your own based on your comprehension and interest in the subject. The other four questions are intended to be answered by the Athletic Advancement/Development administrator.

For the Sport Management/Sport Administration academic program administrator:

- Is there a specific course or an "elective" course a student can take specifically on sport fundraising? If yes, what are the topics and/or subject matter in the sport fundraising course? If no, to what extent is sport fundraising covered in the course of study (i.e. a sport finance or economics of sport course)?
- Is the Sport Management/Sport Administration academic program COSMA accredited?
- To what extent does the sport management/sport administration program administrator(s) perceive the importance of "practical experience"? If cited as important, among which segments of the sport industry (i.e. professional sport, college athletics, high school athletics, youth sport) do most students gain their practical experience?
- Is there a relationship and/or reciprocal arrangement between the sport management/sport administration academic program and the fundraising arm of the athletic department on campus (i.e. the Athletic Advancement/Development office)?

For the Athletic Advancement/Development administrator:

- Based on their educational background, did they ever take specific coursework or an "elective" course on sports fundraising in college? If yes, can they generally describe the topics and/or subject matter from the sport fundraising course? If no, to what extent was sport fundraising covered in their college course of study (i.e. a sport finance, sport marketing or economics of sport course)?
- Are they members of any national professional organizations such as the Association of Prospect Researchers for Advancement or A.R.P.A, and/or the National Association of Athletic Development Directors or N.A.A.D.D.? If yes, have they ever taken any courses

or seminars on sports fundraising? If no, do they plan on joining or is there another professional organization of which they are members?

- During their college years, were they required to complete "practical experience" in terms of practicum hours and/or internship requirements? If yes, among which segments of the sport industry (i.e. professional sport, college athletics, high school athletics, youth sport) did they gain their practical experience?
- Is there a relationship and/or reciprocal arrangement between the Sport Management/Sport Administration academic program and the Athletic Advancement/Development office?

Exercise 2: for practitioners

Based on the chapter lesson regarding data mining and curriculum development attempt to answer the following areas of inquiry.

- To what extent does your Athletic Advancement/Development office utilize data mining and/or predictive analytics? Are you familiar with or do you have practical experience using the following tools?

  A SQL or Structured Query Language

  B ArcGIS (Geographic Information Systems)

  C Experian QAS or Quick Address Software

  D MS Excel spreadsheet, graphs and charts

  E MS Powerpoint, Access and Word

- Based on your educational background, did you ever take specific coursework or an "elective" course on sports fundraising in college? If yes, can you generally describe the topics and/or subject matter from the sports fundraising course? If no, to what extent was sports fundraising covered in your college course of study (i.e. a sport finance, sport marketing or economics of sport course)?
- If your degree was in a Sport Management/Sport Administration academic program, was your college/university COSMA accredited?

- Are you a member of any national professional organizations such as the Association of Prospect Researchers for Advancement or A.R.P.A, and/or the National Association of Athletic Development Directors or N.A.A.D.D.? If yes, have you ever taken any courses or seminars on sports fundraising? If no, do you plan on joining or is there another professional organization of which you are a member?
- Is there a relationship and/or reciprocal arrangement between the Sport Management/Sport Administration academic department and your department?
- What is the likelihood of considering a collaborative project with the Sport Management/Sport Administration department?

REFERENCES

CHAPTER I

ESPN.com (2004) "ESPNU to launch on '03–04–05'", available at http://sports.espn.go.com/ncaa/news/story?id=1951755 (accessed 01/31/12).

Howard, D. and Crompton, J. (2004) *Financing Sport* (2nd edn), Morgantown, WV: Fitness Information Technology.

Kelley, D. J. (2002) "An analysis of differences between gender, experience and school size regarding the responsibilities of interscholastic athletic directors", Ohio University, available at http://search.proquest.com/docview/305523272?accountid=2909 (accessed 01/31/12).

NAYS (2011) "Recommendations for communities", available at http://www.nays.org/CMSContent/File/nays_community_recommendations.pdf (accessed 01/31/12).

NFHS (2011) "High School Sports Participation Continues Upward Climb", available at http://www.nfhs.org/content.aspx?id=5752 (accessed 01/31/12).

Seiler, T. L. (2003) "Developing and Articulating a Case for Support" in Tempel, E. (ed) *Achieving Excellence in Fundraising*, San Francisco: Jossey-Bass, pp. 49–58.

Shapiro, S. L. (2008) "Donor loyalty in college athletics: An analysis of relationship fundraising and service quality effects on donor retention", University of Northern Colorado, available at http://search.proquest.com/docview/304541022?accountid=2909 (accessed 01/31/12).

CHAPTER 2

Bailey, D. (2000) "Women in Sports: Seeking Balance", in Gerdy, J. R. (ed) *Sports in school: The future of an institution*, New York: Teachers College Press, pp. 102–114.

Bonnette, R. M. and Daniel, L. (1990) "Title IX Athletics Investigator's Manual", *ERIC Digest*, available at http://www.eric.ed.gov/PDFS/ED400763.pdf (accessed 01/31/12).

DeLench, B. (n.d.) "Youth Sports Organizations: Six Ways to Increase Accountability, Transparency. Self-regulation doesn't always work", available at http://www.momsteam.com/successful-parenting/community-oversight-of-private-youth-sports-programs-needed, (accessed 01/31/12).

Gerdy, J. R. (2000) *Sports in school: The future of an institution*, New York: Teachers College Press.

Kelley, D. J. (2002) "An analysis of differences between gender, experience, and school size regarding the responsibilities of interscholastic athletic directors", Ohio University, available at http://search.proquest.com/docview/305523272?accountid=2909 (accessed 01/31/12).

Litsky, F. (1999) "Football; NCAA puts Notre Dame Football on Probation", available at http://www.nytimes.com/1999/12/18/sports/football-ncaa-puts-notre-dame-football-on-probation.html (accessed 01/31/12).

Lyras, A. and Hums, M. A. (2009) "Sport and social change: The case for gender equality", *Journal of Physical Education, Recreation & Dance*, 80 (1) 7–8, 21, available at http://search.proquest.com/docview/215755394?accountid=2909 (accessed 01/31/12).

Popke, M. (2008) "High School – Booster Club Guidelines Guard Against Embezzlement", available at http://athleticbusiness.com/articles/article.aspx?articleid=1730&zoneid=9 (accessed 01/31/12).

Prevosto, J. (2009) "Creating a Positive and Effective Working Relationship with Your Booster Club", available at http://www.nfhs.org/hstoday (accessed 01/31/12).

Scruggs, J. (2004) "Grothe confesses to $75,000 embezzlement", available at http://www.dailyhelmsman.com/news/grothe-confesses-to-75-000-embezzlement-1.1850668#.TyfCvFyDvqU (accessed 01/31/12).

CHAPTER 3

Conway, D. (2003) "Practicing Stewardship" in Tempel, E. (ed) *Achieving Excellence in Fundraising*, San Francisco: Jossey-Bass, pp. 431–441.

Gene Smith Biography (2010) available at http://www.ohiostatebuckeyes.com/genrel/smith_gene00.html (accessed 01/31/12).

Kelley, D. J. (2002) "An analysis of differences between gender, experience, and school size regarding the responsibilities of interscholastic athletic directors", Ohio University, available at http://search.proquest.com/docview/305523272?accountid=2909 (accessed 01/31/12).

—— (2000) "Sponsors pay so students can play", *SportBusiness Journal*, available at http://www.sportsbusinessdaily.com/Journal/Issues/2000/12/20001211/No-Topic-Name/Sponsors-Pay-So-Students-Can-Play.aspx (accessed 01/31/12).

Riley, M. B. (2006) *The Ivory Tower and the Smokestack: 100 Years of Cooperative Education at the University of Cincinnati*, Cincinnati, OH: Emmis Books.

Stier, W. F., Jr. (1999) *Managing sport, recreation and fitness programs: Concepts and practices*, Boston, MA: Allyn & Bacon.

The V Foundation for Cancer Research (2010), available at http://www.jimmyv.org/ (accessed 01/31/12).

CHAPTER 4

Birkholz, J. M. (2008) *Fundraising Analytics*, Hoboken, NJ: John Wiley & Sons Inc.

Burlingame, D. F. (2003) "Corporate Giving and Fundraising" in Tempel, E. (ed) *Achieving Excellence in Fundraising*, San Francisco: Jossey-Bass, pp. 177–187.

Conway, D. (2003) "Practicing Stewardship" in Tempel, E. (ed) *Achieving Excellence in Fundraising*, San Francisco, Jossey-Bass, pp. 431–441.

Maxwell, M. M. (2003) "Individuals as Donors" in Tempel, E. (ed) *Achieving Excellence in Fundraising*, San Francisco, Jossey-Bass, pp. 161–176.

Seiler, T. L. (2003) "Developing and Articulating a Case for Support" in Tempel, E. (ed.) *Achieving Excellence in Fundraising*, San Francisco, Josey-Bass, pp. 49–58.

—— (2003) "Plan to Succeed" in Tempel, E. (ed) *Achieving Excellence in Fundraising*, San Francisco, Jossey-Bass, pp. 23–29.

Stier, W. F., Jr. (2001) *Fundraising for Sport*, Boston, MA: American Press.

Weinstein, S. (1999) *The Complete Guide to Fundraising Management*, New York, NY: John Wiley & Sons Inc.

Wylie, P. B. (2004) *Data Mining for Fundraisers*. Washington, DC: Council for Advancement and Support of Education.

CHAPTER 5

Dunlop, D. R. (2002) "Major Gift Programs" in Worth, M. J. (ed) *New Strategies for Educational Fundraising*, Westport, CT: American Council on Education and Praeger Publishers, pp. 89–104.

Fish, M. (2009) "Athletic survival? Get well-endowed", available at http://sports.espn.go.com/espn/print?id=4762882&type=story (accessed 01/31/12).

Hathaway, T. (2003) "Richard Lindner Pledges $10.2 Million to Varsity Village", available at http://www.uc.edu/News/NR.aspx?ID=307 (accessed 01/31/12).

Howard, D. and Crompton, J. (2004) *Financing Sport* (2nd edn), Morgantown, WV: Fitness Information Technology.

Schubert, F. D. (2002) "Principal Gifts", in Worth, M. J. (ed) *New Strategies for Educational Fundraising*, Westport, CT: American Council on Education and Praeger Publishers, pp. 105–111.

Stier, W. F., Jr. (2001) *Fundraising for Sport*, Boston, MA: American Press.

UCATS New Member Referral Program (n.d.), available at http://www.ucats.net/new-member-referral-eachone.html (accessed 01/31/12).

UCATS Priority Points System (n.d.), available at http://www.ucats.net/priority-points.html (accessed 01/31/12).

Weinstein, S. (1999) *The Complete Guide to Fundraising Management*, New York, NY: John Wiley & Sons Inc.

Wylie, P. B. (2004) *Data Mining for Fundraisers*, Washington, DC: Council for Advancement and Support of Education.

CHAPTER 6

Cebrzynski, G. (2007) "Burger King, Denny's go national with high school sports sponsorships", *Nation's Restaurant News*, available at http://nrn.com/article/burger-king-denny%E2%80%99s-go-national-high-school-sports-sponsorships (accessed 01/31/12).

King, B. (2010) "High School Sports Running on Empty", *SportsBusiness Journal*, 13 (15), pp. 1, 15–19.

Kyriacou, C. (2010) "Design flaws in Inglewood school gymnasiums", *The South Los Angeles Report*, available at http://www.intersectionssouthla.org/index.php/author/1482 (accessed 01/31/12).

McFarland, A. J. (2002) "What's in It for Us? Rethinking Corporate Sponsorships in Interscholastic Athletics", Education Resources Information Center (ERIC) document (ED465738), available at http://www.eric.ed.gov/PDFS/ED465738.pdf (accessed 01/31/12).

NAYS (2011) "Recommendations for communities", available at http://www.nays.org/CMSContent/File/nays_community_recommendations.pdf (accessed 01/31/12).

NCYS (2011) "Report on trends and participation in organized youth sports", available at http://www.ncys.org/publications/2008-sports-participation-study.php (accessed 01/31/12).

Sneath, J. Z., Hoch, M. R., Kennett, P. A. and Erdmann, J. W. (2000) "College Athletics and Corporate Sponsorship: The Role of Intermediaries in Successful Fundraising Efforts", *Cyber Journal of Sports Marketing*, available at http://fulltext.ausport.gov.au/fulltext/2000/cjsm/v4n2-3/sneath42.htm (accessed 01/31/12).

Stier, W. F., Jr. (2001) *Fundraising for Sport*, Boston, MA: American Press.

Sports Image Inc. Mission Statement page (2010), available at http://www.sportsimageinc.com/mission.php (accessed 01/31/12).

Webb, C. H. (2002) "The Role of Alumni Relations in Fundraising" in Worth, M. J. (ed) *New Strategies for Educational Fundraising*, Westport, CT: American Council on Education and Praeger Publishers, pp. 332–338.

CHAPTER 7

Ammon, R., Jr., Southall, R. and Blair, D. (2003) *Sport Facility Management: Organizing Events and Mitigating Risks*, Morgantown, WV: Fitness Information Technology Inc.

"High School Licensing Program: Time to get in the game" (2010) *High School Today*, available at http://www.nfhs.org/content.aspx?id=3524 (accessed 01/31/12).

Howard, D. and Crompton, J. (2004) *Financing Sport* (2nd edn), Morgantown, WV: Fitness Information Technology.

Irwin, R., Sutton, W. and McCarthy, L. (2002) *Sport Promotion and Sales Management*, Champaign, IL: Human Kinetics.

Muret, D. (2010) "Michigan expected to name Sodexo as concessions vendors", available at http://m.sportsbusinessdaily.com/Journal/Issues/2010/03/20100329/This-Weeks-News/Michigan-Expected-To-Name-Sodexo-As-Concessions-Vendor.aspx (accessed 01/31/12).

NCAA (2008) "2004–2008 Revenues and Expenses of Division I Intercollegiate Athletic Programs Report", available at http://www.ncaapublications.com/productdownloads/RE09.pdf (accessed 01/31/12).

Popke, M. (2009) "Merch madness: A new nationwide licensing program could help high schools generate new revenue and protect their image", available at http://athleticbusiness.com/articles/article.aspx?articleid=2601&zoneid=34 (accessed 01/31/12).

Revoyr, J. (1995) *A Primer on Licensing*, Stamford, CT: Kent Press.

Rowell, D. (2002) "Sports fans feel pinch in seat (prices)", available at http://espn.go.com/sportsbusiness/s/2002/0621/1397693.html (accessed 01/31/12).

SportsBusiness Journal (2006) "Dotting The Eyes: OSU Tops Home Depot's College Paint Sales", available at http://www.sportsbusinessdaily.com/Daily/Issues/2006/09/Issue-11/Sponsorships-Advertising-Marketing/Dotting-The-Eyes-OSU-Tops-Home-Depots-College-Paint-Sales.aspx (accessed 01/31/12).

SportsBusiness Journal Daily Article (2009) "The Swamp: Florida's home field advantage", available at http://www.sportsbusinessdaily.com/Journal/Issues/2009/08/20090824/SBJ-In-Depth (accessed 01/31/12).

Steinbach, P. (2010) "Colleges Use Social Media to Sell Sports Tickets", available at http://athleticbusiness.com/articles/article.aspx?articleid=3599&zoneid=40 (accessed 01/31/12).

Stier Jr., W. F. (2001) *Fundraising for Sport*, Boston, MA: American Press.

The Associated Press (2006) "Longhorns hook record merchandising revenue", available at http://sports.espn.go.com/ncaa/news/story?id=2562097 (accessed 01/31/12).

Trademarks and Licensing General Information (n.d.), available at http://www.uc.edu/licensing/general_information.html (accessed 01/31/12).

CHAPTER 8

Birkholz, J. M. (2008) *Fundraising Analytics*, Hoboken, NJ: John Wiley & Sons Inc.

Carlson, M. (2000) *Team-based fundraising step by step: A practical guide to improving results through teamwork*, San Francisco, CA: Jossey-Bass Publishers.

Hodge, J. M. (2003) "Gifts of Significance" in Tempel, E. (ed) *Achieving Excellence in Fundraising*, San Francisco, Jossey-Bass, pp. 89–102.

Martinez, J., Stinson, J., Kang, M. and Jubenville, C. (2010) "Intercollegiate athletics and institutional fundraising: A meta-analysis", *Sport Marketing Quarterly*, 19 (1) 36–47.

Nudd, S. P. (2003) "Thinking Strategically about Information" in Tempel E. (ed) *Achieving Excellence in Fundraising*, San Francisco, Jossey-Bass, pp. 349–365.

Stier Jr., W. F. (2001) *Fundraising for Sport*, Boston, MA: American Press.

Strout, E. (2007) "Courting female donors", *Chronicle of Higher Education*, available at http://chronicle.com/article/Courting-Female-Donors/7396 (accessed 01/31/12).

Williams, K. A. (1997) *Donor focused strategies for annual giving*, Gaithersburg, MD: Aspen Publishers Inc.

Worth, M. J. (2002) "Elements of the Development Program" in *New Strategies For Educational Fundraising* Westport, CT: American Council on Education and Praeger Publishers, pp. 11–23.

CHAPTER 9

Catalog of Federal Domestic Assistance start-page (2011), available at https://www.cfda.gov/ (accessed 01/31/12).

Grace, K. S. (1997) *Beyond fundraising: New strategies for non-profit innovation and investment*, New York, NY: John Wiley & Sons Inc.

The NFL Youth Football Fund (2011) "NFL Grassroots Program 2011 Request for Proposals (RFP)", available at http://www.nflyff.org/pdf/2011_Grassroots_RFP.pdf (accessed 01/31/12).

CHAPTER 10

Brassie, S. (1989) "A student buyer's guide to sport management programs", *Journal of Physical Education, Recreation and Dance*, 60 (9) 25–28.

Fuller, D. (2002) "Data mining overview", available at http://www.information-management.com/newsletters/analytics-data-mining-predictive-ROI-value-10021815-1.html (accessed 01/31/12).

Hjerpe, K. L. (2009) "The absence of technology in undergraduate sport management curriculum and its relationship to intercollegiate and professional athletics", Robert Morris University, available at http://search.proquest.com/docview/305167663?accountid=2909 (accessed 01/31/12).

Kelley, D. J. (2002) "An analysis of differences between gender, experience, and school size regarding the responsibilities of interscholastic athletic directors", Ohio University, available at http://search.proquest.com/docview/305523272?accountid=2909 (accessed 01/31/12).

Kreutzer, A. L. (2000) "The education of sports administrators", in Gerdy, J. R. (ed) *Sports in school: The future of an institution*, New York: Teachers College Press, pp. 66–73.

Laird, C. (2003) "Perceptions of sport management curriculum and the NASPE NASSM approval process: An analysis of undergraduate sport management academicians", Ohio University, available at http://search.proquest.com/docview/305319440?account id=2909 (accessed 01/31/12).

Luperchio, D. (2009) *Data mining and predictive modeling in institutional advancement: How ten schools found success*, Washington, D.C.: Council for Advancement and Support of Education.

Newell, W. H. and Klein, J. T. (1996) "Interdisciplinary studies into the 21st century", *The Journal of General Education*, 45 (2), 152–169.

"Sport Management Programs: United States" (2011), available at http://www.nassm.com/node/96/print (accessed 01/31/12).

Stier Jr., W. F. (1993) "Alternative career paths in physical education: Sport management", *ERIC Digest*, available at http://www.eric.ed.gov/PDFS/ED362505.pdf (accessed 01/31/12).

—— (2001) *Fundraising for Sport*, Boston, MA: American Press.

Zaman, M. (2005) "Predictive analytics: The future of business intelligence", available at http://www.mahmoudyoussef.com/BI/9.doc (accessed 01/31/12).

INDEX

Page numbers in *italics* refer to illustrations.